PASSIO

SEX

PASSIONATE
SEX

DISCOVER THE SPECIAL POWER
IN YOU

DANIEL S. STEIN, M.D.

with Leslie Aldridge Westoff

CARROLL & GRAF PUBLISHERS, INC.
NEW YORK

Illustrations by Frank H. Netter, M.D. Reprinted with permission from *The Netter Collection of Medical Illustrations, Vol. 2.* Copyright © 1954, Novartis. All rights reserved.

Illustrations by Daniel S. Stein, M.D.

Interior photographs by Romulo Yanes

First Carroll & Graf trade paper edition 2000

Carroll & Graf Publishers, Inc.
19 West 21st Street
New York, NY 10010-6805

Library of Congress Cataloging-in-Publication Data is available.
ISBN: 0-7867-0705-4

Manufactured in the United States of America

To my mother and father,
Pat and Bill Stein,
Whose lifelong romance
Personified the vital connection
Between love and mind, body and spirit,
Who taught me by their living example
The true meaning of
Love and commitment.

Disclaimer

Readers are advised to consult with a health-care provider knowledgeable in reproductive medicine and sexual issues for advice regarding their particular health and sexuality needs.

This book is intended to be an inspirational guide based on sound medical experience; however, it is not intended to substitute or replace the counsel of qualified professionals.

Acknowledgments

To my thousands of female patients and their loved ones who entrusted me not only with their physical care but with the totality of their emotional well-being. They shared with me their everyday frustrations and sexual problems and inspired me to write *Passionate Sex*.

Colleagues whose personal teaching and living examples inspired my writing include Dr. Deepak Chopra, the late Dr. Eduard G. Friedrich, Jr., Dr. Hugh Shingleton, Dr. Bruce Dooley, Dr. Don Carrow, Drs. Barry and Nan Seedman, Dr. Dick Neubauer, Dr. Aaron Hasiuk, Dr. Len Haimes, and Dr. Louise Campbell.

Friends without whose warmth, love, council, advice, encouragement, and support this book could not have been written include Dr. Jack and Jane Fisher, Catherine Winter, Becky Bolletti, Stacy Hopkins, Barbara Federspiel, Dr. Kathryn Stieh, Tom Gordy, Kim Rose, Dijana Belegu, Cindy Ward, Dr. Michael and Angie Resnick, Debbie and Ed Kuhnel, Susan Greenwood, and Carol Kaplan.

To Will and Phoebe Ezell for showing not only the geniune affection of their friendship, but their numerous excellent ideas and constructive criticisms.

To Donna Kingman for her creative suggestions and constant support of this project and me.

To Dr. John Gagnon without whose Renaissance mind, scholarly thought, and steadfast belief in me and in the value of this effort, this book would never have been written.

To Dr. Cathy Greenblat and Suzanne Sloan, who believed collectively in this project and me, and both of whom spent countless hours editing and contributing to this manuscript.

To Ed Venner and Dick Keogh of Ventel Corp. for their help and patience, their expertise and commitment to make the manufacturing of GyneFlex perfect.

To David Pettis for his counsel and always sound advice. To Tim Opfer for helping a novice to function effectively in the computer age.

To Jack Hazelton for his amazing talent of guiding the crafting of ideas into graphics that communicate a visual impression that is clear, understandable, and beautifully articulate.

To Romulo Yanes, talented principal food photographer of Condé Nast's *Gourmet,* for creating amazingly beautiful and non-threatening photo images of toys. To Jack Descent for his belief in this project and the work yet to come.

To Andrew Tarr and Hudson Young for reminding me of the importance of music.

To Jerry Ellis and Lou Off who brought exercise physiology to the forefront of my consciousness, by appointing me Executive Medical Director of Sportslife. To Gary Carleton and George Schyder who appointed me Medical Editor of *Vie Magazine.* The experiences of learning and teaching with them led me to follow through with developing the GyneFlex for Love Muscle exercises.

To my agent, Mitchell S. Waters of Curtis Brown, whose faith in me as a writer guided me to the successful completion of this effort.

To my publishers, Kent Carroll and Herman Graf whose enthusiasm, consistent cooperation, and sound advice made publishing this effort successful. No one could wish better guidance and support from a publisher. To Martine Bellen whose answers to every imaginable production question helped make this book. To Jodee Blanco for her seemingly limitless enthusiasm, boundless energy, and valuable ideas.

Every book is a collaborative effort as the acknowledgments above indicate. Thus, I am grateful to many people. However, there is one person who stands out above all the rest. To Leslie Aldridge

Westoff, who helped me fashion ideas into words, who was constant in her patience with my focused effort to communicate clearly and memorably, to make this contribution the best it could be.

Daniel S. Stein, M.D., F.A.C.O.G.
New York, New York

Contents

Contents

Introduction

I have written this book because of a crucial need I see in society today. At times there seems to be a frightening lack of mental, physical, and spiritual health. As a physician, I have dedicated my life to healing, to helping to make the world a better place. My search for wisdom in medical, psychological, and spiritual areas has caused me to blend modern traditional medicine with the best that I have found in my extensive experience in healing knowledge. From this emerged my ideas about the mind/body/spirit connection to loving sexuality that fill the following pages.

I was trained at Wayne State University Medical School in Detroit and practiced traditional medicine for more than fifteen years. During that time I saw many thousands of patients in my office, in the comprehensive women's medical center I established and ran, and in several hospitals. I often realized there were many things that I could not do to heal their pain, however much I wanted to.

I also realized how important to life and death simply touching my patients could be. I vividly recall the case of another doctor's wife who lived in Florida. I had done a simple vaginal hysterectomy on Thursday and, as we had previously discussed, had left on Friday for a two-day medical meeting in New York. Early Sunday morning I got an emergency call from the hospital in Florida. My patient had taken a turn for the worse and seemed to be dying.

I took the next flight back and went straight to the hospital. I found her with massive abdominal distention, irregular heartbeat, complaints of severe abdominal pain, and with her blood electrolytes completely out of whack. I examined her and sat talking to her with my warm hand on her abdomen for some time while I reassured her and told her I was staying in town and would see her twice a day until she was better.

The next day I was able to disconnect her IV fluids and two days later she went home pain-free. And all I did was touch her and tell her she would soon be better.

Because of this and similar incidents, I began to explore ways to broaden my approach and expand my knowledge. I studied yoga and Reiki (a school of healing touch of which I am a Master), spent considerable time with the great Satguru (highest caliber of Indian spiritual teacher), Paramahamsa Hariharananda, became a certified clinical hypnotherapist, and studied aromatherapy, color therapy, and music therapy.

I spent time studying with doctors of divinity, naturopathy, hyperbaric oxygen therapy, and chiropractic medicine. I became a member of the American College for the Advancement of Medicine. And bit by bit, I merged the lessons of these rich medical traditions with knowledge of formal medical school training and residency in obstetrics and gynecology to create better ways of healing.

That background and my patient experience have led me to one of the most important discoveries of my career . . . a new vision of the role sexuality and love can play in promoting health and longevity. The reason I am taking this sexual approach is because its role as a fundamental healing aspect of life is either being ignored or has never been recognized by our society.

Who should read this guide to loving sexuality? It is written for:

1. Couples who already have a strong commitment.
2. Couples who are in the process of developing a loving relationship.
3. Singles who are hoping to have a loving relationship.
4. Singles or couples who already have a good sex life but would like to learn new ways to enrich it.

I believe that by following the suggestions I offer, you will be able to channel the vast potential of your sexual energy in directions that *prevent* illness and lead to a *longer,* more joyous, productive, healthier life. We don't need a Renaissance, the revival of old sexual mores and standards; we need a Naissance, the birth of a new sexual culture where bonded couples give and accept the profound healing energy of love.

Part One

The Importance
of Being Sexual

Chapter 1

The Healing Power
of Your Sexuality

Our sexuality is perhaps the most powerful source of healing energy we possess. Yet sexuality has also long been a major source of human tragedy. Out-of-control sex has been the reason for a multitude of sins. Whether a power for good or ill, sexuality has played an important role in the development of human life.

Loving sexuality reflects the vital connection between mind, spirit, and physical action. It is a relationship that is so basic that nurturing it will help you to improve the quality of every aspect of your life in unimaginable ways. When I say loving sexuality, I am not talking about the spiritual communion of two minds. And I'm not talking about the mental communion of two spirits. We are not disembodied minds and disembodied spirits, but we are whole human beings—mind, body, and spirit rolled up into one. In order to reach the spirit and mind of your committed partner in health-promoting ways, you must have loving behavior. You have to be sexual. Properly understood, loving sexuality is an art that expresses the highest levels of mental and spiritual union, respect, and cherishing.

It is always a positive force. It brings not only immediate physical and emotional gratification, better self-esteem and confidence, and spiritual rewards, but perhaps most important, *better health and a longer life.*

Loving sexuality is about increasing the intensity and ecstasy in your lovemaking and bringing extraordinary intimacy to a relationship. It is about sharing, giving, receiving, and stimulating pleasure, and integrating your mind and spirit into your loving. It is not just a tonic for tired relationships; *it is medicine in its most holistic, broadest terms.*

As Dr. Dean Ornish has written in his best-selling book, *Love and Survival,* "Love and intimacy are at the root of what makes us sick and what makes us well, what causes sadness and what brings happiness, what makes us suffer and what leads to healing. If a new drug had the same impact, virtually every doctor in the country would be recommending it for their patients. It would be malpractice not to prescribe it. . . ."

I believe that loving sexuality is a medically identifiable method for healing our bodies of illness, our minds of stress, sadness, and depression, and as a source of inspiration for our spirits. In the process it will also help transport us to a universe of joy and pleasure some of us never knew was attainable. Your sexuality need not be an element within you to be feared, as religion and parents may have taught some of you, nor the taboo certain parts of society may have taught others. It need not be obscene, dirty, or sleazy, as those who profit from pornography portray it. Our sexuality is a vital, healthy part of each one of us when channeled for good.

We talk about improved nutrition building and healing the cells of our bodies; the importance of aerobic exercise circulating healing oxygen to our hearts and brains; the role of yoga and meditation in cleansing, focusing, and healing our minds; the significance of faith in inspiring and comforting our spirits. But until now we have not understood the enormous importance sexuality can, and should, have in our lives. When we think, we use only a fraction of our brain power. We breathe with only a fraction of our lung power. And so also, we use only a fraction of our sexuality because we have never been taught to understand the many healing and wonderful things it can bring.

Learning to increase the positive power of your sexuality to change your life and make it healthier, happier, and longer, will enable you to clearly identify what you want for yourself, and to create extraordinary improvements in the quality, purposefulness, and results of everything you do.

Connected Loving

The advantages of being connected to loving sexual actions reveal themselves on three levels: body, mind, and relationships:

1. **Body**—you will see startling effects on your body such as an enhanced immune ability to fight external invaders like bacteria and viruses; to repel internal invaders like cancer cells; to lower blood pressure; to improve the oxygen-carrying ability of your circulatory system; and for better metabolic and hormone balance.
2. **Mind**—you will learn how to visualize your desires, choose what you value, and apply the resulting energy and focus to your intention to create change for yourself and the world around you. You will learn to use your mind to make a difference in your life.
3. **Relationship**—you will find closeness and intimacy, trust and respect, by being one hundred percent there and valuing being there. You will make a difference in others' lives by example. You will know both the joy of love as well as the fruits of love, friendship, and bonding with others.

By reading these chapters you will learn how to connect to your highest values so that your physical and sexual acts are directed by logic and reason, wisdom and goodness, love and desire . . . all in unison. You will learn how to create a universe where your loving sexuality becomes different from just sex. We are all capable of both. But sex for the sake of sex alone is isolating because your body is performing an act of love without involving your heart and mind.

By contrast, a loving sexuality gives life to your spirit. It puts the actions of your body in sync with your mental and spiritual values. It is an expression of the bond that exists between two people who feel strongly, live vibrantly, and commit to mutual passion. Loving sexuality brings a heightened clarity to your vision of the world.

Sex in this context is the healthiest of all activities because it is not only the physical union of two people but the expression of spiritual loving. It is basic and close to the heart of existence from which all creativity and life itself springs.

The Result of Making the Right Connection

When your sexuality expresses your mind and spirit, you will find that you have more vigor and vitality; more enthusiasm for family, work, and community; more self-respect and self-fulfillment. By connecting to a vibrant sexuality you will sense a feeling of lightness, exuberance, control, self-empowerment, and excitement about life:

1. You will know the profound bliss and ecstasy of sexual pleasure.
2. You will know the deep satisfaction of feeling close to another human being.
3. You will enjoy a healthier mind and spirit resulting in a healthier body.
4. You will think more clearly.
5. You will experience self-gratification, enhanced self-

esteem, and be more confident about trying new things.

6. You will see the aging process begin to slow.
7. You will begin to understand and control your life's purposes.

A Journey up the Staircase

You may be surprised to learn, as you read and grow, that you are on a journey of discovery. Like most journeys, it is not only the destination that is important but how you get there. The mastery of each step up the staircase enhances your health, happiness, and joy in life. As you take it, you will explore yourself, open your mind to new possibilities, see your sexuality in exciting new ways, become uninhibited, responsive, and fantastically orgasmic. You will discover a new vision of yourself. Your dreams and desires will generate the energy to focus and make things happen.

We live in a world built on energy. Couples who learn to incorporate a healthy sexuality into their loving will increase their life energy. They will climb an imaginary staircase to higher levels of emotional and spiritual evolution.

Good sex produces energy. Bad sex loses it.

Loving sexuality in bonded couples produces a joyous relationship that is expanding, creative, and ultimately fulfilling. The steps I will give you are new ideas that will help your sexual relationship become more physically rewarding, to blossom anew each season into something more beautiful and more spiritually gratifying.

The longer it lasts, the better it gets.

The Need for Energy

Without the conscious and constant input of positive energy, all structures from buildings to relationships, from flower gardens to whole cultures become disordered and decay. This is what happens so often in relationships between women and men. The positive energy of loving sexuality is rarely expressed or is lost over time, to be replaced by the energy-sapping experiences of loveless sex and guilt. Without this effort, many relationships descend the staircase as loving sexuality disappears, or, worse, never appears.

By learning to understand your sexuality and use it in productive ways, you will help heal the gap that exists for so many couples in contemporary society between your dreams and your daily life. These recommendations are for you. You take them into your mind, digest and absorb them with logic, intuition, and will, until they become part of you. That is easy enough to say, but it means we each have to examine who we are, visualize what we want to bring into our lives, and how we desire to live in the third millennium.

To find a better quality of life, you have to start here and now. You must start with yourself. Certainly you can be happy without great sex. But you are living only a fraction of the joy in life that can be yours. You are not filling your lungs. And you lose out on that tremendous rejuvenating boost to your health that loving sexuality can bring you. With a creative sex life you can tap into the enormous potential of that fundamental wellspring of energy.

Our desire to have sex is not only so we can create children to protect the survival of the human species. Because most of us have only two children, that would happen only a limited number of times in our lives. Despite the importance of reproduction, it is not the complete reason for sexual love. Sex at its best is the ultimate way to enjoy and celebrate life itself. The will to merge your sexuality and the desire to commit to sharing your life with one other human being is true love. It is a miracle that it can ever happen in our supersaturated, techno-media world offering seemingly limitless options. But if you live by the principles I suggest and open your hearts and minds, *it will happen.*

Because I am a physician, many women have come to me looking for a solution to mental, physical, and emotional problems that are rooted in their either having never discovered their own sexuality or having lost touch with it. I have repeatedly been asked for practical advice they could turn to so they could enjoy and improve their sex lives. These patients asked me for a key to opening their natural childlike curiosity for sexual exploration that has been buried in a mysterious, dark compartment in the mind that has been closed and locked for years.

They have browsed through sex manuals in stores and read self-help books, but there was nothing that pulled it all together. No book or tape offered them a view of sexuality as the complete mind/body/spirit connection. A connection that is so rewarding in terms of personal health. A love-sex connection that reinforces an ever stronger union with another human being. People are healthiest when their sexuality directly reflects their mental and spiritual identity.

Ask yourself these questions. How many people do I talk to every day who tell me their life is full of bliss and delight? How many can say they are happy?

I don't hear it. I look around at the world today and I see stress, depression, isolation, and sexual confusion. Sexual misconduct from adolescents to adult leaders is so widespread, it could almost be considered normal. I see patients, couples, even friends and family who want and need help to become healthy.

How It Works

How can you develop the kind of loving sexuality that we all seek? This guide will help you learn to:

1. Accept, understand, and love yourself more.
2. Develop a better knowledge of men's and women's bodies and your own body.
3. Intensify your senses . . . your conscious receptivity to touch, taste, sound, smell, and sight.
4. Share as much of your emotional self as you can with

your loved one to build a bond of spiritual intimacy. Strengthen, enliven, and enrich your mental union by communication and shared experience that builds trust, the infrastructure of emotional love.

5. Recognize that a loving sexuality emerges from relaxed, playful, uninhibited enthusiasm. This attitude needs to be encouraged in some, enhanced in others, and developed in those who treat sex as a silent act to be gotten over with quickly. Time, imagination, and communication have to be devoted to it.

6. Nurture and prize the loving, sexual aspect of your relationship. Give it constant energy input, prepare for it, and savor it each time as a special occasion.

7. Cultivate an attitude that bodies are not something to be ashamed of. They are to be loved, adored, respected, and cherished.

We all have the enormous untapped power to learn how to improve our lives. If you don't make the effort, if you continue to look only under rocks, you will find only worms and salamanders. If you look up to the heavens and reach for something lofty, you will find rainbows and treasures of gold.

You are never too old to change. The ideas I offer you are at once both timeless and ageless. They are not meant for any special period of your life. They are meant for all your life. They are not meant for our particular age in history. They are universally applicable from the dawn of mankind to the end of existence as we know it. The more people who connect to healing and being healed by their sexuality, the healthier our culture will become.

Now take the first step up your energy staircase through sexual spiritual discovery. Choose healing intimacy to bring you vibrant good health and joy in life.

Chapter 2

The Medical Connection

It doesn't take too great a stretch of the imagination to believe that anything as wonderful and pleasurable as your sexuality can be the missing link to healing the woes of your mind and the ills of your body.

But it is probably more difficult to believe my theory that the quality and frequency of your sexual acts can have a medically measurable effect on your body, actually curing some diseases and preventing others; or that loving someone sexually can affect how long you live. It's all true. The miracle of how this is possible, as you will see, is through the mind/body/spirit connection.

My new approach to health and longevity is healing through sexuality. It is an approach that has never before been popularized, let alone by a physician and gynecologist.

While we are more concerned than ever with vitamins, nutrition, and gym workouts to promote fitness and longevity, sexuality is the most important pathway to health, yet it is something we don't think about, talk about, or even recognize.

Millions of people are suffering because they cannot establish or maintain a committed mind/body/spirit relationship. The ability to care about, understand, and commit to another person, only one of six billion on our planet, is a dream which too many of us hope for in vain.

As you read this book, I will provide you with a medical doctor's arsenal of ideas to help you see your sexuality in different terms, to help you use it as you have never used it before—as a positive, life-enhancing route to better health, greater happiness, and a longer life. You will open your mind and be able to heal the hurt of past problems and discover new worlds. You will begin a journey that will last for the rest of your life.

The time to make the effort is now. The need is urgent, because the longer you fail to prioritize your sexuality, the further removed you will be from its healing potential. The longer you deprive your body, mind, and spirit of sexual fulfillment, the harder it will be to change, to wake it up and know joy, as well as to create a deeply satisfying sex life. If you have a relationship worth improving or saving, now is the moment to act before bad habits become ingrained and lead to a steady decline down that staircase.

Finding Your Mind/Body Connection

To rescue your sexuality from misinformation and confusion, to turn it into the unique force for healing it can be, we have to look at the extraordinary connection between our minds and bodies.

When you realize how emotions and thoughts can change how your body feels and responds, you will understand how a positive, dynamic part of your being such as your sexuality can be so instrumental in keeping you healthy. You will see that something that you believe, or an emotion sensed by your brain, can have a direct effect on your body's systems and their ability to fight disease.

If you wonder how strong the mind/body connection is or whether it really exists, I can offer you many examples:

1. The husband of one of my patients wanted to stop smoking. He tried everything and nothing worked. Then he went to a hypnotist who programmed his subconscious mind not to want to smoke, to find it distasteful. He never smoked again, thus overcoming addiction.

2. One woman was so stressed at her office because of friction with her boss that she developed a terrible rash on her skin and only by changing jobs could she get rid of it. It disappeared as mysteriously as it had come.

3. A man was so upset about the gyrations of the stock market, he started having violent headaches that he had never experienced before, and had to go to a psychiatrist. The headaches disappeared when new attitudes developed with counseling. No medicine was needed for this complete cure.

4. There was a woman I remember who was so tense about trying to get pregnant and have a child before her biological clock ran out that she could not conceive. Finally, she decided to adopt a baby and she mentally relaxed. It was at that point that she instantly became pregnant. Not only is ovulation suppressed by stress, but a woman's hormone system in general is affected as well. For example, it frequently happens that young women will skip periods in times of pressure such as when they first start college, during exams, or when they are worried about becoming or being pregnant.

5. A woman told me of an incident that took place when she was a teenager. To have some fun, her boyfriend surprised her by stroking her right underarm delicately and gently. Unexpectedly she had a strong orgasm. It was her brain that received the impulses from her arm and sent them down to her

genital area to create the feeling of orgasm, though her boyfriend had never touched her there. The mind/body connection once again.

6. In patients with heart disease, studies have shown that feelings of sadness or tension may double the odds that the coronary arteries will narrow, causing a temporary but potentially dangerous drop in the blood supply to the heart. Thus deprived of oxygen, heart attacks can occur.

7. People who live with pets, mostly dogs or cats, have less hypertension and longer lives.

8. Death or divorce can be devastating causes of long-term depression due to the loss of love.

9. Having to care for an Alzheimer patient causes some to become so depressed, it has in turn led to their own illness.

10. If you are in love and that love is not returned, just watch for these physical symptoms: insomnia, weight loss, stomach cramps, colds, irritability, and so on.

There are endless stories that prove your mind relates to all of your body. Many recent studies in psycho-neuro-immuno endocrinology have dramatically shown that the links between your mind, your nervous system, your immune system, and your endocrine system are so strong that the lack of a healthy relationship to basic positive things in your life can lead not only to depression but to seizure disorders, ulcers, migraines, infections (bacterial and viral) hormone imbalance, diabetes, abnormal bleeding, heart attacks, high blood pressure, and cancer.

Stress Research

There is an overwhelming amount of evidence that suggests there is a mind/body link that can both permit and prevent disease. The brain's thought and emotional centers are capable of regulating virtually all the aspects of the body's immune and endocrine defense mechanisms that have a profound effect on health.

Studies being done at Carnegie-Mellon University in Pittsburgh have found that people suffering from long-term stress lasting at least a month and coming from a serious problem such as divorce, having difficulties with relatives or friends, or a job loss are statistically more likely to catch a cold than others. The higher the stress score, the more likely the person would become ill when exposed to a virus.

In another recent study, Carnegie-Mellon psychologist Dr. Sheldon Cohen and colleagues at the University of Virginia Health Sciences Center exposed 276 healthy people to cold viruses and found that those with the most ties to family, friends, and community were least likely to become sick.

Looking further into the effect of stress on the body, Dr. Cohen found that being under severe stress for more than one month but less than six months doubled a person's risk of viral infection. Severe stress lasting more than two years nearly quadrupled the chances of getting sick.

In observing my patients, I have found that bad sex or no sex produces stress, which in turn causes illness. This leads down the energy staircase. Good loving sex reduces stress, fights illness, and takes you up the staircase.

Tricking the Mind

New medical research using placebos now dramatically shows how strong the relationship is between the brain and the rest of the body. Telling the mind that something is being done, even though it isn't, can alter our cells, tissues, and organs almost as if by magic. Some of the studies are hard to believe, but they are very real.

Take, for example, the research doctors in Texas conducted on patients needing arthroscopic surgery on their painful knees. In some patients the surgery was actually performed. In others, small cuts were made in the knee as though the surgery had been performed, but nothing at all was done.

Two years after surgery, patients who had the fake operation reported the same relief from pain and swelling as those who had actually had the operation. In other words, what the brain expected would happen caused the body to make happen.

A simple study in Japan was done on thirteen people who were extremely allergic to poison ivy. Each person was rubbed on one arm with a harmless leaf they were told was poison ivy. The other arm was rubbed with a leaf of real poison ivy that they were told was not. What happened?

All thirteen people in the study broke out with a rash on the arm that had been rubbed with a harmless leaf, and eleven of the thirteen did not get a rash on the arm that had been rubbed with the real poison ivy leaf.

In a fascinating study at Tulane University Hospital Center for Sexual Health, Dr. Eileen Palace used a placebo to make women who had never had an orgasm feel aroused. She connected the women to a machine that supposedly measured their vaginal blood flow, or arousal. After showing the women things that would excite the average person, she told them the machine indicated that they had, in fact, become aroused. They hadn't, of course. But as soon as she told them they had, their brains took the information and went to work so that they did show an actual increase in their vaginal blood flow.

The New Medicine

Medicine, whose primary task is to heal, is being forced to change its attitude about health. Drugs and surgery used to be the only answers and still are the traditional accepted treatment for disease. But medicine is moving away from a focus on "cure," partly because of an increasing demand by patients toward a focus on preventive medicine, life enhancement, and longevity. Studies now point not only to the treatment of disease, but how to change the way we live to prevent it.

This new field has been called integrated medicine because it combines traditional cures with holistic or alternative medicine. In my mind, this means treating a human being as a whole. It is not treating just a disease in a person, but treating a person who has a mind, a body, and a spirit. All of these need to be addressed in order to prevent or treat disease and to accomplish ideal health. This is medicine with a heart and soul.

The trend toward seeking preventive advice or alternative medical treatment such as acupuncture and hypnotism has exploded in the nineties. Harvard researchers report that it has risen by nearly fifty percent in this decade, with eighty-three million Americans, more than forty percent of the adult population, using it. And more than half our medical schools now include courses in alternative medicine meant to complement traditional treatment.

However, when a patient is seriously ill, most doctors still turn to a specialist in that disease. Only rarely do they acknowledge the enormous creative potential of engaging the mind, emotions, and spirit in the healing process, or of integrating the usual procedure of drugs and surgery with the new alternative approach of healing the whole person and the pattern of his or her living such as nutrition, exercise, social relationships, habits, beliefs, past experience, and future expectations.

Important centers of research such as the Duke University Medical Center are discovering that traditional medicine alone does not cure all patients. They find that "lifestyle and psychosocial factors" play an important role in preventing and curing illness, especially chronic illness. Research centers across the country are sponsoring studies in hypnosis, meditation, yoga, acupuncture, Reiki, dance, breathing techniques, massage therapy, healing touch, aromatherapy, color and music therapy, magnets, and off-site prayer.

At Duke, before Dr. Mitchell Krucoff operates on his cardiac patients, a request for prayers is e-mailed or phoned to Buddhist monks in Nepal, a Carmelite convent near Baltimore, an interdenominational center in Missouri, as well as several other places. Although the results are too statistically small to be definitive, Dr. Krucoff has found that the outcomes of those prayed for were fifty to one hundred percent better than those who were not prayed for.

Harvard University has a medical affiliate specializing in spiritual medicine, and researchers around the country are using music as medicine for the mind and body. Two therapists in Texas found that pregnant women who listened to music were only half as likely to need anesthesia. At Colorado State University it was found that stroke victims who were treated with music improved their ability to walk. How does it work? Supposedly, music helps strengthen the nerve cell connections in the brain, which then influence the rest of the body.

The Immune System

The immune system, which we use to prevent and fight disease and is so affected by feelings of chronic stress, pain, depression, and hopelessness, is a vast network of interrelated cells and chemical messenger substances as well as nerve fibers in the thymus gland, lymph nodes, bone marrow, and spleen. When you suppress or bottle up your emotions such as your sexual longings, and become sad, depressed, or isolated, you are also suppressing your immune system and increasing susceptibility to disease.

How? When you suppress your immune system, you decrease the number and activity of disease-fighting white blood cells and natural killer cells that are produced. These are the body's natural defenses, which are capable of destroying bacteria and viruses as well as tumors.

Natural Killer Cells

It sounds like natural killer cells ought to have horns, spears, or lethal weapons. In fact, they look like ordinary cells, but they have the capacity to function as regulators of the immune system, the blood-building system and the neuroendocrine or hormonal system. They roam the bloodstream looking for alien cells to attack. The more we have of them, the better. And guess what? Their numbers and activity are stimulated by loving sexual activity, relaxation, humor, and pleasure, as well as by nutrients such as beta-carotene, vitamins C and E, pycnogenol, zinc, argenine, garlic, and echinacea.

Stress and Sexuality

When you starve yourself by doing without sexual loving, you create and maintain in your subconscious mind a state of perceived inescapable danger. This sense of danger is caused because you are blocking the natural tendencies of humans to bond, and you feel isolated.

When this natural innate need of all human beings to be with another person freely, with love, orgasms, joy, and happiness, has been squelched by repression, unhealthy restrictions, or lack of interest and opportunity, the body is continually frustrated and sees this as a threat to life.

When stress is perceived by the brain, the response immediately goes to the immune system, the hormonal system, and the nervous system as the body goes into full alert to survive. It stops everything and focuses all its resources on escaping danger by preparing the body to fight or flee. It stimulates the adrenal cortex to produce corticosteroids, which energize the body to combat the danger. The primary one is cortisone.

However, cortisone is also used to prevent organ rejection in people with transplants. It is a very potent supressor of that immune system, which you need to be healthy. So when your brain is alerted to perceive life-or-death danger, it lowers all the body mechanisms that ordinarily protect you from viruses and bacterial infection, which it senses as a lesser danger. But when you are not sexually stressed, when you are enjoying and fulfilling your natural desire for loving sex, you will produce the opposite situation. All your healthy defense systems integrate and operate at full speed.

I am suggesting that it is possible for you to experience a very real health change by becoming sexually fulfilled and finding love and joy in your life. You eliminate the chronic stimulation of your adrenal gland, which produces immune-suppressing steroid hormones. Not only that, but you enhance, by direct nervous stimulation from your brain and from your emotional centers, crucial things like the production and activity of needed white blood cells and natural killer cells, the enhanced production of antibodies, more efficient food metabolism, and more efficient scavenging of free radicals, which cause aging of the body and may be a primary cause of cancer.

So we have the stressful emotions, which are deprivation, isolation, anger, and fear, and the comfort emotions, which are love, pleasure, and sex. The comfort emotions make you better and are healing because you get rid of the hurtful emotions and associated suppression or dysfunction of your vital systems and you add the positive benefit of the health-enhancing stimulation of these same systems.

Sexuality and Cancer

I believe there is a strong relationship between the increasing rate of cancer in this country and lifestyles that promote unhealthy chronic and acute stress rather than a healthy, loving sexuality. What we are doing is literally stressing ourselves into a reduced defense against cancer.

Cancer cells are constantly being formed in our body every day. Because of the huge number of normal cells that are dividing, the chance that one of those cells will undergo some kind of division accident, whether caused by dietary factors, a virus, heredity, all three, or something else, is certain. It is estimated, for example, that women form new breast cancer cells every day from the age of eighteen on.

It is also suggested that women will not develop breast cancer unless there is some breakdown in the efficiency of the natural killer cells in their immune system that normally would destroy cancer cells as they develop. The precancer cells destined to become cancer lose the ability to stop growing (growth restraint) and become wildly disorderly. Normal cells know when to stop growing. For example, if you get a cut, it heals to the edges and the normal cells stop growing when the cut is healed. These precancer cells are like overgrown bushes. They don't stop. And they crowd out and compete with other nearby cells for oxygen and nutrients. Even worse, when they gain the ability to spread or metastasize to distant sites such as the lung, bones, and brain, they have become cancer.

This is why cancer in a twenty-five-year-old man or woman is so often much more aggressive and dangerous than in a sixty-five-year-old person. The sixty-five-year old has had years of a properly functioning immune system that has offered protection for a long time, which is a sign that the natural killer cells have worked effectively and efficiently and are likely to continue.

But when a twenty-five-year-old immune defense system fails and cancer develops, the immune system is really not as strong as if it had protected the person until late in life, and cancer takes over more rapidly.

Contrast this with a situation where there is a healthy committed relationship, where there is sexual joy and happiness, and where the excess stress-generated adrenal production of cortisone and cortico-steroids is reduced. Instead, your life-promoting and life-enhancing sexual happiness stimulates the production of those natural killer cells and their strength, activity, and effectiveness, and stimulates the effective production of antibodies and the healthful integrated functioning of the hormone and immune systems.

This does not mean that sexually happy people don't develop cancer. I am suggesting that with more natural killer cells and a stronger immune system, some people may have a better chance of preventing it.

Sexual satisfaction and pleasure with a loved partner also stimulates the brain to create endorphins, which reduce the sense of pain, allow you to metabolize oxygen better so that every cell functions more efficiently, and send positive messages to all your body cells that you want to live, that life is fun, that life is joyous.

Sexuality and Living Longer

As you have seen, if you are happy and your mind, body, and spirit are functioning harmoniously, stress and disease are diminished, and all your systems hum along in peak form. When you are enjoying a loving sexuality and you take into your consciousness new ideas and new ways of looking at things, you will actually change your belief system and take actions that allow you to live longer.

If your sex declines, your life declines. If you believe
in the positivity of your own existence and reinforce
it all the time with loving actions, *you will be
healthier and you will live longer.*

There is a growing body of evidence to support my conclusion
that if you allow your sex to decline, you allow yourself to age more
quickly and shorten your life. The idea of living longer because we
have better sex seems much more fun than overdosing on herbal
pills or prescriptions that might or might not work. Recent research
has shown that contrary to the old notion that sex is a drain on
life's forces, it actually does increase the life span. And the greater
the number of orgasms, the greater the probability of a longer life!

A 1997 study reported in the *British Medical Journal* by Smith G.
Davey and colleagues examined the frequency of sexual intercourse
and death in a sample of nine hundred men ages forty-five to fifty-
nine over a period of ten years.

In the group having the highest number of orgasms, mortality
rates were fifty percent lower than the group with the lowest frequency of orgasms. Interestingly, results were even more dramatic
in those men with coronary heart disease. Those who had orgasms
about twice a week had a sixty-eight percent lower death rate than
those who had them less than once a month. The researcher suggested that hormonal effects on the body resulting from frequent
sex might explain the findings.

While for men the number of times they had sexual intercourse
affected their rate of longevity, in studies on women it was the
quality of the sex they had that seemed more important in their
longevity. Further studies in both sexes are planned.

Sexual Loving

Sexual loving helps eliminate the extraneous aggravating circumstances and trivialities that accrue during the day to create a kind of low-level stress that is unhealthy. I don't believe the universe intended us to have depressing, miserable lives. I think the universe intended us to be happy, joyous, creative, and helpful to the world and the people around us, most important our loved ones and ourselves.

By getting vitally in tune with your sexuality, you use it to spark creative ideas. Your sexuality elevates your very being. Mind and spirit work together to bring the health, happiness, and longevity we all seek. When love and pleasure lead to hope and optimism, which cause all systems to function in an integrated, positive, and life-enhancing manner, the result, as we have seen, is extraordinary. The mind and spirit soar on wings of love.

There is no question about the existence and medical importance of the mind/body/spirit interaction. There is no question about the existence and medical importance of the mind/body/spirit connection to loving sexuality. I call this the Vital Connection because it is so basic and fundamental in its contribution to health and longevity.

Becoming Integrated

When your loving is connected to the rest of you, you function as a whole. You learn healthy patterns of living. For example, you find time for sex, for exercise, for planning and eating a balanced diet, and for being with your children. You develop a better attitude and relationship with your work, friends, and the world around you. You smoke and drink less or not at all. You eat healthily, knowing the nutrients of your food are the building blocks for healthy cells tomorrow. But learning this, as with all knowledge, begins with self-knowledge.

Once you are able to shed any negative associations about sex that come from misinformation, conditioning, hurtful past experience, embarrassment, or self-consciousness, you can move forward to the fulfillment of fabulous loving, terrific orgasms, and the miracle of intimacy that is a reflection of all the energy and fire in your enlightened intellect and your soul.

How Much Sex Is There?

With all the advantages of a loving sexuality in mind, the need for us to rethink our approach to sexuality is crucial. The fact that most of us don't give enough attention to understanding and enjoying our sex lives is abundantly clear when you look at the divorce rate. If fifty percent of marriages fail, a higher rate than in any other country, there must be a key element that is being ignored. If we devote more time and thought to working, eating, shopping for clothes, watching TV, and surfing the Net than we do to understanding the basic bonding between men and women and fulfilling our hunger for love, then something is wrong.

No, sex does not need to be lurid, shameful, indecent, or embarrassing, nor does it have to be hidden from or whispered about. It is a powerful force within all of us to be used to enhance our lives, to help us flourish, to nourish our minds and spirits.

As Robert T. Michael, John H. Gagnon, Edward O. Laumann, and Gina Kolata have pointed out in the most comprehensive survey of American sexual behavior of the 1990's *Sex in America*. "Anyone looking at the allusions to sex that surround us every day would have to conclude that sex is an American obsession."

This may be true, but they also observe that we are "a society full of desires that fail to be realized." There just isn't as much sex going on as people think there is.

- The most sexually active people are married couples, and only forty-five percent of them have sex a few times a month, which isn't very often; one third have sex with their partners only a few times a year or not at all; and only eight percent have sex with their partners four or more times a week.

- Singles who are not living with a partner are having great sex, right? Wrong. Only twenty-five percent of them, says the study, have sexual intercourse a few times a month and another twenty-five percent have it only a few times a year. It seems clear that a healthy sexuality is missing from a lot of lives. By healthy sexuality, I don't just mean sex the physical act. I mean the ability to connect to your mind and spirit so your body overflows with positive life energy. I mean loving sex. The point is not to have *meaningless* sex, which can cause stress and isolation, but to have *meaningful* sex, which produces joy and intimacy. They are quite different.

Unfortunately, because sex is such a heavily charged subject in our society, sometimes so difficult to discuss and learn about, the many sexual problems most people face from time to time, and some people face almost all the time, are not dealt with effectively. This is unhappy as well as unhealthy.

The Case of Mary

One of my patients, for example, was nineteen and had a fairly religious Catholic upbringing. Mary went to church every Sunday with her parents. When I saw her she was living with her lover, something which in her mind was wrong because she was not married. She was making love without the intention of having a child, and was using the contraception I prescribed. She felt guilt and shame and could not enjoy their sex as much as she wanted to. And she was too embarrassed to discuss her problem with her partner.

Every time she went to church she felt worse. She got progressively more depressed, lost weight, got sick a few times, and finally was willing to talk to me about it. What I did was sort through her fears and gradually help her come to an understanding that from a health, wellness, and medical point of view, her behavior was a disconnection of her mind and body.

Showing her a way to live a life that was in harmony with her beliefs and her sexuality was really more important than all the Prozac, antidepressants, sleeping pills, and tranquilizers I could have prescribed.

She either had to stop having sex so she could live her spiritual values or she could read, think, and discuss enough to change her belief system and accept her own sexuality in a context that was different from that of her upbringing.

If she wanted to learn, grow, change, and find a way out of her depression, she would have to consciously say "These values are not those I choose to have anymore. These new values are the ones I choose to live by. When my heart is with a man I love, I will be free to make love to that man. I will choose what I value and value what I do."

Live Your Values

If your sexual behavior does not reflect your values, it will often have a major impact on your health, frequently leading to depression.

Clinical depression strikes more than seventeen million Americans each year, according to the National Institute for Mental Health. It is the second leading medical expenditure in this country ($47 billion a year to treat) and the leading cause of illness in women. It is also responsible for other diseases, because when you are stressing your body by not doing what you believe, your immune system, hormone system, and nervous system become as involved as your mind and you end up taking a series of drugs.

Drugs may cover up problems. They rarely cure them.

We have inherited enormous negative influences on the subject of our sexuality, which encumber us with obsolete ideas. Not only are we in need of spiritual and intellectual awakening to heal so many of the sex-related issues that bother us at home and in the office, we remain very much in the dark with regard to knowledge of our sexual selves.

We frequently operate on the basis of fallacious or incorrect assumptions.

Some of us never realize even after years of sexual relationships with one or more partners that our sexual "knowledge" can be just plain wrong.

Where the Ideas Come From

We get our attitudes about sex from parents and relatives, and what they say and do at home; from our friends and fellow classmates who give us information and misinformation, for they may be ignorant and crudely hurtful; from religious institutions where it can be ill-founded and repressive; and from television, videos, and films. We live in a society where the apparent worship of sexy celebrities, sexy entertainment, sexy advertising, romance novels, pornography, and topless bars fill the need for the love that is missing from so many adult lives. It is rare to see a true fusing of love and sex in TV and commercial films. Most films do not show us romance as the fulfillment of love and as a natural expression of a person valuing another human being, respecting them, cherishing them, and loving them spiritually.

There are few films that show us how rewarding it is to have a job that makes you happy and have a joy-filled life with your wife and children where your actions are a reflection of your spiritual and mental values. Abusive sex, sleazy sex, casual sex, sex as comedy, sex in cyberspace, or sex used as a power tool in an interpersonal control drama is sold to us as far more entertaining. It's the same commercial sensationalism that operates in newspapers. Good news is thought to be boring. It is not dramatic, scary, colorful, or entertaining, so little of it gets reported. With all this coming at us, we continue to be confused over what Real Sex is all about, how to make contact with it, and what to do with it.

So, how do you begin to find that vital connection from mind and spirit to sex and health?

This book gives you the tools for continual personal growth and learning. Your mind will open to finding and exploring your sexuality, thus preparing you to understand the detailed love techniques in Part Two and Part Three, which you can use to ensure a healthy sexuality, heal many of your problems, and help to avoid the dangers of stress, depression, isolation, and illness. You will learn how to take new ideas of sexual intimacy and combine them with your own to create a situation where boredom, that killer of so many relationships, doesn't have an opportunity to thrive. You will bring healthy, loving sexuality into your daily living, elevating and inspiriting your heart and mind, and drawing to you, as if magnetically, a wealth of life-enhancing events, people, and pleasant surprises.

I cannot overemphasize the importance to both women and men of a positive attitude. Ignite your loving sexuality to discover joyful, healthy, and healing energies.

From earliest life we have a need for love, intimacy, and the warmth of human contact. But supposing you can't find the right person to bond with, to sexually adore, the soul mate of your dreams. Then what do you do?

You love yourself.

And if you *have* found the right person, you still must begin by loving yourself. You cannot give what you don't possess. Only when you know and love yourself can you truly give love to your partner.

Chapter 3

Discovering Your Self

We are all born with the natural potential to be great lovers. But these are learned skills. They are neither intuitive nor hereditary. Few, if any of us, have benefited from a formal education in sexuality, loving, or how to create and maintain a successful lifelong relationship.

I don't think anybody does anything sexual using intuition. We transfer from one experience to another the knowledge we gain about sexuality from past loving experiences that form the basis of what we do. It may seem like it's intuitive when we move a certain way, but it is probably based on some experience we've had that has taught us that particular move is going to be fun.

The Sexual Split

Once you acknowledge the desire to learn, if you can remove distractions and focus the energy of your desire on the intention to change, to become the real you, you will, by the time you have finished this book, have found out how to have spectacular loving sex along with enhanced self-esteem, and more confidence about trying new things in sex, as well as in the other important areas of your life.

Desire focused by conscious intention creates the power to change and improve your life.

We all deserve to have pleasure, create it, and enjoy the most cherished and sacred things our bodies and minds are capable of imagining.

It simply doesn't make sense to splinter our minds and bodies. It is laughable to see movies and prime-time TV shows that are full of explicit sex, read romance novels where heroines enjoy the love many women seek but cannot find, to see endless erotica on the Internet and sex headlines on the cover of every major popular magazine, to be bombarded by sexy ads and billboards, and then to turn around and be frigid and as disinterested as possible in improving our own personal sex lives.

The gap between what we want and what we do is enormous.

The gap between what we know about most things and what we know about the interconnection of sex and love with our immune system, hormone system, nervous system, and healing mechanisms is unacceptable.

Women have always said if men were the ones who had babies, the perfect contraceptive would have been discovered long before now. In the same way, it seems to me that if past generations had dealt more positively and acceptingly with human sexuality, the taboos and stern warnings that have kept us from learning about love and sex as a force for spirituality and growth would long ago have vanished.

The Power of Connecting

Our lives are made up of a series of connections. To begin with, there is the Primal Connection, the umbilical cord attaching us to life in our mother's womb. Next come the things we see in our nursery, our teddy bears and our parents. Later on it's becoming attached to our friends and school. In our jobs the connection we make to our colleagues is called networking. All along the way we create a myriad of links, but all of them are influenced by the mind/body connection, which is so powerful, and the spirit, which can lift us from the ordinary to the extraordinary.

To find value in life, we must look deep within ourselves to the very fundamental life-promoting things that help us. For example, if we get more involved with our work, our work didn't change, our attitude toward it changed. Merging with our basic sexuality affects our behavior, values, deeds, actions, judgments, and perceptions.

What happens when all the things that are unhealthy and distance people from one another prevent us from bonding? What happens when we are unable to enjoy compassion, touching, and the sensitivity and responsibility of intimacy? We become isolated.

If we don't make our right relationships, we live the life of a recluse.

One of the greatest causes of stress-related disease is isolation or the feeling of not being involved with anyone.

The more significant are our connections, the richer and healthier are our lives.

But while many of the things we do don't bring us closer to intimacy, not nearly as close as two people sitting drinking a glass of wine in a Paris café in springtime, there are more opportunities for reaching out now than we ever have had in the history of civilization. Which also means there are so many more opportunities to make mistakes when you act without thinking.

By taking the techniques you learn and the energy you get from making contact with your sexuality, you go from directionless to purposeful. You focus on what you want to do sexually. Being there sexually means you are right there for your relationship, for intimacy. You transfer subconsciously, and sometimes consciously, what you have learned into nonsexual activity in other areas of life. You learn to concentrate on the here and now, and that ability helps

you to think more clearly and remember the values you have chosen to make important.

Each time you make positive things happen in your world and recognize that you can make a difference, you gain life energy and move up toward optimum psychic, spiritual, and physical health.

If you are out of shape and try to climb a steep staircase rapidly, you will find the experience is both exhausting and frustrating. With practice and patience, the steps you climb by making positive things happen bring energy to your life and make further ascent easier and easier.

Reaching out to your sexuality, your basic core creative energy of life, is tremendously healing. It is healing to discover yourself as a sexually integrated mind/body/spirit.

The single greatest antidepressant is choosing a direction toward a better life.

You get up and get out of the house. You do something. You are not just treading water. You have direction. You make judgments about whether people or activities are positive, healthy, and happiness-promoting, or stressful, anxiety-promoting, and drive you crazy. You disengage whenever possible and without guilt from people and activities that make you feel bad. You have a Program Against Depression. You're **doing** things and life is getting better.

Staying Sexually Healthy

In our world of specialists, healers offer different solutions to those who need help. Physicians, ministers, counselors, psychologists, psychiatrists, nutritionists, chiropractors, naturopaths, teachers, and social workers all have good ideas.

Yet a great deal of healing goes on outside the offices of these experts. You are healed by your positive relationships with parents, children, friends, and lovers. Particularly your lover, the person who should be closest to you, privy to your most intimate self, the person who knows more about you than anyone else in the world, because in a healthy, safe, trusting, healing relationship, you have opened yourself to that person.

Sexual healing means not just making love together (disconnected sex), but experiencing meaning together (vitally connected loving sexuality).

If you live on disconnected sex, fantasy sex, sleazy or violent sex—these ingredients become your sexual mind and body. You corrupt and degrade love, your spirit drops, and your relationship with significant others founders. The loss is yours.

What I propose to you is a pathway you can take to an optimum, loving sexuality. But this is not all. Learning to enhance your loving sexuality teaches lessons that you can use to make the rest of your life better, more productive, less stressful, and happier. Loving sexuality leads to wellness in general. It creates in you an aura of positive life force that you radiate to the world. This health-promoting loving sex produces an *energy surplus* that you can apply to produce positive results in all areas of your life.

Finding Happiness

Many people are deeply disturbed about their sexuality and their intimate relations. The huge numbers of unhappy and frustrated people are astounding. The stampede to Viagra by both men and women certainly indicates a widespread desire to improve the sexual compartment of their lives, which I support. We seem to be getting progressively more distant from the healthy roots of life.

We seem to have become a culture that values money more than love. What we do, look for, and even think we want are not necessarily coming from where our minds and hearts are.

We need to connect to the values of an enduring civilization.

We each have to find a better quality of life and reestablish a code of values we believe in. To do this, you have to start at home. Start with yourself. Make yourself healthier and happier.

Certainly you can be happy to some degree without a great sex life. But it's experiencing only a part of the happiness that could be there for you. It's not going to give you the opportunity for better health that could totally rejuvenate you. Or you can have a purely sexual relationship which may be tension-releasing but will do nothing else for you. It will not be elevating in a mental and spiritual sense. With a fully developed sex life, you tap into the fundamental wellspring of the vibrational energy of human nature. Without it, you are trying to run a race with only one shoe.

But if you become happier because you have made an effort to understand your sexuality, you are happier within yourself. Your ability to impact the world around you and to touch others' lives in a positive and healing fashion is greatly enhanced because you yourself have begun the process of healing the inhibitions that have distanced you from the true expression of your creative soul.

Then, the person you have sex with must be someone you value, respect, and admire. Someone you connect with in a visceral sense, so you have the mental, spiritual, emotional, and physical all working together. You are not trying to make it (impress, enchant, conquer) with a series of different people. When you relate to your values, you are always with someone you want to be with. You are never in a stressful, fearful, or dangerous situation because you are always with a person you trust. To value the person you live with, and the people you work with, and your friends, you must first value yourself. You must know yourself intimately.

What follows are directions and specific instructions in a variety of sexual techniques that will forever keep your sex life vibrant, entertaining, and creative, and open your imagination to new physical acts that support the love that is there. Look upon the tools I offer you as more exciting techniques of lovemaking than you may ever have considered. They will invigorate your relationship and go a long way toward curing depression, healing illness, and promoting good health, and a long life.

Won't more information on sexual technique only lead to more sexual calamities, unwanted pregnancies, single parents, and sexual misconduct?

No.

It doesn't work that way.

Ignorance leads to directionless dissipation and action because you can neither value anything nor evaluate it, since you don't have the knowledge to make an informed judgment. The more information and control you have, the more opportunity there is for making the right choices.

When you discover new knowledge of your body or your partner's body, or a novel way to play in bed, you will be able to enjoy a fulfilling and expanding world that keeps you young and alive. There will be fireworks that come from a dynamic, colorful, relationship that reinforces your loving sexuality with each moment of tenderness, each touch, each orgasm.

You may love someone deeply emotionally and mentally but after all those years be so turned off physically, you both end up having affairs and your relationship breaks up and it's all because you didn't keep the sparks alive, the vital juices flowing to every cell in your body, immersing you in the energy of a healthy life. And that life energy is your sexual energy. We are conceived of sexual energy. We are born from it.

The Case of Stanley and Dolores

There is a businessman I know who had an affair with a younger woman, as so many wandering middle-aged men do. Stanley had been married for many years and had three children. He loved his wife, Dolores, valued and respected her. But gradually he became aware of the fact that she was increasingly low key and quiet, while his job demanded that he be very energetic. Soon they were on such different rhythms, they stopped having sex.

She had become tired of the sameness of the things they did and stopped putting out energy. Dolores had her man, she'd produced children, and she became overconfident about their relationship. She no longer felt she had to maintain her body and beauty. She never exercised and gradually allowed herself to gain weight. She never read a book and there was no personal growth, nor did she pursue any interests in common with her husband. Mentally and physically she was no longer the person he had fallen in love with.

Stanley saw what was happening, lost his attraction to his wife, and stopped putting his energy into the relationship as well. That vicious cycle led them to break up when they were supposed to stay together for a lifetime. In divorce there is no winning.

When Stanley made the decision to cut himself off from his wife sexually, he also cut off the energy that was sustaining their relationship, and there was nothing left to bring it to life again. There is little chance Dolores will ever do something sexually that she hasn't done before, unless they make something happen. That is why it is so important to be able to heal yourself through your sexuality and invigorate your life. Without new sexual energy coming into a relationship, the union becomes a half-life for both. With it, there is no limit to what partners can do together.

Harold's Life

In another case, a couple I treated shed their shared shyness and inhibitions. Harold explained that after reading some books, thinking about what he'd read, and as a result discovering ways to become a more romantic lover, he had become so sexually connected to his wife, and it was so energizing, he was able to do ten times as much as anyone he knew. As he told me: "It was because I had with me, every moment that I lived and breathed, in my heart, the love of this human being that I valued above life itself. That I respected more than I respected anyone. Whose innocence and ingenuousness and integrity were the greatest in the universe. Who was the embodiment of everything I cherished, loved, and adored."

The depth and fulfillment of Harold's sexual love for Angela is what created the energy to inspire him and make him so successful.

This can be you. But even if you decide not to try anything new, the mere reading of what follows will have the effect of changing you by exposing you to new adventures. The process of bringing into your consciousness new insights will forever alter the course of every action you take. As you live them, think them, and make them part of yourself, these insights will peel away layer by layer, the barriers to understanding universal truths.

You cannot remain the same person once you have begun to move up the staircase. You have nothing to lose and everything to gain.

Part Two

Finding Out
Who You Are

Chapter 4

Getting to
Know Yourself

To enable yourself to change so you can discover your sexually loving nature, you have to make contact with the person you are and the person you want to be. Sometimes they are one in the same. More often they are not. To find out, you must learn to visualize the dreams of this ideal person who is you.

Preparation

To begin this task, you need to clear distraction from your mind. If you are like most people, you will probably be thinking about six things at once, such as when you have to pick up the kids, business meetings you musn't forget, calls to make or errands to run, your tennis date Saturday morning.

When such thoughts begin to intrude, gently but firmly cast them from awareness.

Now ask yourself with regard to your own self-image: "What do I desire?"

I'm not talking only about the physical self you see in a mirror, or the sexual self that is part of you. I'm talking about the self you are as a *whole* being. Your mind, your body, your sexuality, and your spirit.

An Exercise in Visualization

What I want you to do is visualize. This means to imagine. This section teaches you how. Pick a moment for yourself every day to practice with privacy, e.g., during your bath.

This is not a random exercise where you let any image pop into your mind like closing your eyes and seeing a sunset.

With your eyes open or closed, open your mind and let yourself think about who you are. Imagine who you desire to be.

Imagination is the ability to create an idea or mental picture. In visualization, you use your imagination to create a clear image of the person you would like to become.

Continue to focus on your vision or notion of yourself regularly. Look consciously and deeply at who and what you are.

See yourself freely and honestly.

Try to form a mental image of what you want for yourself. Do you want a long and healthy life full of freedom, laughter, self-awareness, curiosity, enthusiasm, wonder, joy, ecstasy?

Do you want all your senses to participate in that awareness?

Do you want to accept your body so that you can enjoy it regularly and discover new and mysterious ways to share the pleasure of your own sensations with your partner?

Imagine yourself enjoying your body.

Imagine yourself comfortable and relaxed within your body.

Imagine accepting your body, disregarding the prejudice and guilt that linger from events of the past, or the hurts from childhood, or from abusive relationships.

When you start accepting yourself, you shed the fears and inhibitions about your sexuality, your body shape, being overweight, your droopy breasts, your small penis, and all the things that embarrass you and make you self-conscious. You shed those feelings that are impediments to happiness and good loving. You understand that your body is just a body, like so many other bodies, some fatter, some thinner, some bigger, some smaller, but all just human, all bound to change with the passage of time.

Visualize yourself making a change that will bring an ever-increasing self-fullfilling, self-enhancing, and self-enriching journey through love and enlightenment.

When we create something, we always create it first as a thought or idea.

This idea always precedes something happening. "I think I'll kiss him" always precedes leaning over and embracing. "I want a new dress or suit" precedes going out and buying one. An inspired architect first has an idea. His visualization of it then results in a set of plans. Your ideas when combined with your own energy create a visual image like a blueprint.

Simply having a picture and holding it in your mind generates energy that will tend to make that image real.

If you constantly think you are ill, you become ill. If you believe yourself to be attractive, you become so. You draw into your life what you think about most, believe in most strongly, expect on the deepest levels, and imagine most vividly. To one degree or another, you create what you expect.

The more positive energy you put into thinking of what you want to be, the more it will begin to happen in your life. The process of change does not occur on a superficial level. It involves delving into and discovering your most basic attitudes about yourself. That's why learning to use visualization can become a process of deep and meaningful growth.

In the process you may discover ways in which you've been holding yourself back, keeping yourself from achieving satisfaction in life through fears and negative self-concepts. Once clearly seen, these limiting attitudes can be removed, allowing you to live in your natural state of happiness and fulfillment, health and love.

Some people wonder what is meant when I use the terms "visualize," or "mental image." Some have worried because they didn't actually see a picture when they closed their eyes and tried to imagine something. Others say they see clear, sharp images in color. Still others just become aware of a feeling or impression. That's perfectly fine. Don't get stuck on the word "visualize." It's not at all necessary to mentally see a picture or image like a photograph. However you find that you are seeing yourself, or feeling something, you are doing it, and what you are doing will work.

If you still really don't feel sure what it means to visualize, try this exercise:

A Practice Exercise

- Close your eyes and relax deeply in a familiar room like your living room.
- Focus in your mind on some familiar detail such as a picture on the wall, or the shape of a chair, just to practice getting a visual image.
- Imagine some pleasant experience you've had in the past few days, especially involving a good physical sensation such as eating a great meal, receiving a massage, making love, even taking a relaxing shower or bath.
- Remember the experience as vividly as possible and enjoy the pleasurable sensations once again.
- Now try to see yourself in some idyllic country setting relaxing on soft green grass on the bank of a tranquil lily-filled pond, or wandering through a beautiful forest in the fall with lots of colorful leaves on the ground. It can be a place you have been or a place you would like to be.
- Think of the details and create it any way you want.

Whatever process you use to bring these images to mind is your way of visualizing.

- Use your conscious mind to program this positive new information about who you are.

If your brain has been programmed by negative thoughts about yourself that you no longer want in your life, then you must reprogram it so you can change.

Program Your Own Reality and Live It Now

Always be positive.

If you program "I'll never be able to have an orgasm," then you won't.

If you program "I can't stand the thought of having (vaginal, oral, anal, any) sex with him," then you won't.

If you program "I have great orgasms," then you will.

If you program "I like all kinds of sexual loving," then you will.

In the province of the mind, there are no limitations.

Learning to reprogram yourself usually comes with experience.

The more you practice it, the easier it will be.

Always think of now.

Think about your images as if they already exist. That is to say, think of what you desire for yourself in the present tense, not in the future.

Don't say "I *will* feel great about my body."

Do say "I *feel* great about my body."

Emphasize what you want, not what you don't want.

Don't say "I'm no longer ashamed of my body."

Do say, "I like my body and feel good about it."

This is not lying to yourself. This is acknowledging the fact that everything appears first on a mental plane. And it can become real most easily by bypassing all the obstacles your mind places in its way.

Keep your images sweet and simple.

Use a few key thoughts or words to trigger these images of how you would like to be, or which role model you would like to emulate.

The Case of Cindy

Cindy, a patient of mine, told me about a special moment she had rather unexpectedly.

"I had the opportunity of traveling to a primitive island in the South Pacific," she said. "It was very beautiful. The empty beaches stretched on forever, the shimmering water was incredibly blue, the fish swam slowly about, almost asking to be seen through my snorkel, and the glistening palm fronds bent gently in the lazy breeze.

"At home I always raced about, locked into my normal daily routine. Up—shower—dress—grab half a breakfast—rush to work. And so on the island I also did what one had to do every day. The difference was, one didn't have to do much of anything. Nothing was going on. And I mean nothing!

"I had fallen into a culture that was totally different from my own. So I stopped and sat and found myself breathing quietly, looking inward, and suddenly I could see myself more clearly than ever before.

"Now everything around me was so basic and simple. Time slowed because I was doing less and thinking less. I could not have found a distraction if I had wanted to."

In that intense state of relaxation, of casting the mundane details of daily life from her cluttered mind, she was able to get a window into herself. She said, "That visit told me where I had been, where I was going, and most of all, who I was, and I didn't like it. I had become someone who wasn't me. I did not hear, see, or smell all the things around me. I was too busy and took it all for granted because it was always there. My mind was a mess. My brain overloaded."

After this spontaneous insight into who she was, she was able to visualize living her own values. She became happier. This happened to her on a South Sea island. But it could have taken place in a park, or woods, or the roof of her apartment building. Or it could happen on a quiet stretch of an off-season beach, wherever you can extract yourself from the world around you, step away, and feel close to nature, and comfortably, quietly alone.

Visualization is the process by which desires are consciously focused into intentions. As I have said, intention energized by desire leads to action, growth, change, and improvement. It takes you up the staircase. To get good at getting better, you must practice every day.

The Case of John

John was an executive in an insurance company. He was a real type-A personality, a workaholic who was driving himself and his family crazy. He was getting progressively more irritable with his wife and children and beginning to have sexual problems he had never had, becoming less responsive to his family, for whom he had less and less time.

He was afraid that if things didn't shape up, he was going to go out and have an affair. Fortunately, before the affair occurred, his wife came to see me.

"Look, Dr. Stein," she said, "I know we need the income from my husband's job, but it's just gotten out of hand. He's a completely frantic man. He's neglecting me and the family. He's out of control."

What had happened was he had lost harmony with himself. His life was hectic, frenetic, bouncing off walls, trying to get things done, meeting deadlines, taking work home with him in the evenings, sleeping fitfully, and waking up thinking about how to make more money and find material success. This is what society made him believe one had to do to be successful.

The way he became aware of what was happening and reconnected with his values was through his wife's help in making the effort to show him that he had become a driven man and to urge him to try visualizing what he really wanted in life, and what they wanted together.

This allowed him to quiet his mind and reestablish his connection to his own soul and to the loving sexuality that had always made life so meaningful. He decided to take a much less demanding job. As a result, he spent more time with his family, had time for a fantastic sex life with his wife, and became a much healthierperson.

Dumping his old self and linking up with the visualized image of who he wanted to be was responsible for John's life change. The alternative would have been drugs and tranquilizers, which would have numbed his senses, dulled his mind, and suppressed his ability to bring his brain and soul back together.

Medication has value.

But *self-discovery* was needed to show John the healthy direction out of his trap.

Once you connect with the basic person you are, you will be a refreshed, enthusiastic, more clear-thinking and balanced person. You will make your own family and office life happier and more effective, and you will have a similar impact on all those around you. Decisions will be easier to make, stress and tension will be reduced, work will be more pleasant, there suddenly will be time for long weekends of loving. The quality of your life will improve. Your sexuality will be awakened. The hurts you live with, like a deteriorating marriage, will be healed.

Take Off Your Mask and Put On Yourself

Let me now go over with you ways in which you can help yourself find out what has happened to the roots of your loving sexuality, choking somewhere under the burden of all the things that have happened to you in your life.

Ask yourself "Who am I?"

Take an honest look at yourself. Stand up and be counted for who and what you are.

Value who you are and accept it.

Now try to identify ways in which you wear a mask and attempt to be someone other than who you are to impress people.

For example, people frequently don masks when they buy cars they can't afford, choose pretentious houses that cost too much, wear designer clothes to flaunt the label, carry designer handbags that are really fake, or flirt outrageously in bars to try to show the world how sexually irresistible they are.

Finding the Real You

I don't want this to happen to any of you, so let's get rid of those masks now.

On the left side of a piece of paper, write down a list of masks that you wear, and on the right side what the real you is like.

For example, you could write:

(Mask) "I drive a Mercedes" ---(Real Me) "I'd rather drive a
                                         Jeep"

(Mask) "I'm a great hostess" ---(Real Me) "I hate company"

(Mask) "I'm sexually shy" ------(Real Me) "I'd love to try
                                         being the aggressor"

(Mask) "I like dieting"-----------(Real Me) "I'd like to eat
                                         everything"

(Mask) "I am happy" ------------(Real Me) "I am bored to
                                         death"

(Mask) "I have great   (Real Me) "I'd love to have
orgasms" --------------------------an orgasm"

Take the paper on which you have made your lists while imagining what kind of person you want to be.

Think positively about each image.

Remind yourself to accept who you are, the Real Me, and achieve a new state of comfort with your physical and mental self.

Spend at least ten minutes twice a day visualizing your real self. Here's how to do this:

Choose an image about yourself that you can easily imagine, like being uninhibited and wildly aggressive.

Sit or lie down where you won't be disturbed.

Get in a comfortable position.

Relax your body completely.

Relax the muscles around your eyes, your head, your neck, shoulders, chest, abdomen, all the way down to your toes. Think of relaxing every muscle in your body, letting all tensions flow out.

BREATHE IN SLOWLY AND DEEPLY FROM YOUR BELLY.

BREATHE IN THOUGHTS OF WHAT YOU DESIRE TO BE.

BREATHE IN YOUR INTENTION.

BREATHE OUT TENSION.

RELAX WITH EACH EXHALATION.

DEEPLY AND EVER MORE DEEPLY RELAX EACH TIME YOU EXHALE.

When you feel completely relaxed, visualize exactly what you would like to be. See yourself and everything happening to you just as you want it.

Imagine any details that make it more real to you. Take as long as you wish.

Have fun with it.

Be like a child daydreaming about what he wants for Christmas.

Keep your images in your mind.

Make some very positive reinforcing statements to Yourself, such as:

"I am a great and thoughtful lover."

"I have a wonderful boyfriend (girlfriend) and we are getting happier and happier every day."

"I am handsome."

"I am beautiful."

"My body is sexually attractive."

"My love life is great."

Since positive statements are very important, what do you do if doubts or contradictory thoughts arise?

Don't resist or try to prevent them. This gives them a power of their own. Just gently let them pass through your consciousness and turn your mind back to your positive visualization.

Continue these exercises for at least three weeks. This may sound like a lot, but any action you repeat daily and consistently for three weeks will become an ingrained part of your subconscious mind and will stay with you for life. You will see it is worth the effort.

Bring the images of who you are without your masks with you to different environments, wherever you go, to parties, the doctor, or the supermarket.

Accepting and valuing your body, your mind, and your own sexuality in different circumstances will help you cast away social pretenses forever and make a real and lasting change.

YOU NOW KNOW WHO YOU ARE.

THINK ABOUT IT AND MAKE IT REAL.

You will see that you have come to a much better state of positive acceptance of yourself and have an expanded sense of sexuality, which you will be able to share with your lover.

As you visualize, remember to:

1. **See yourself as happy and fulfilled**
2. **With your body that's as good as anyone else's**
3. **With your mind that is as valuable as anyone else's**
4. **And with your soul that's capable of soaring as high as anyone else's.**

As a doctor, I have seen bodies big and small, fat, hairy, flat, and frail. I assure you, however, that the happiest people I've seen have simply let go of their masks and embraced their visualizations. They have given up trying to be what they are not. They've made a decision to accept who they really are and to connect with themselves. And once they have recognized this, they are able to begin the thrilling journey of bonding with their lovers, their friends, their family, their children, and accepting the processes of life: aging and change.

They become one with the sexual, the spiritual, the intellectual, and the universal life forces of nature.

By universal life forces, I mean the energy all around you—in the plants that grow and give off the oxygen you breathe, the animals that are part of your world, the ground you touch with your feet, and the water in the ponds and rivers. These are the things your molecules come from, molecules you share with the universe.

Did you know you change most of the billions of molecules in your body every ninety days? You are not made up of the same molecules you were ninety days ago. I am talking of the entire body. Your brain cells. All your cells. Some are not new cells, but the molecules (the clusters of atoms) in them are all new.

The foods you eat today are literally the building blocks for your cells. That's why nutrition is so important. But when you seek a happier, better, healthier, and longer life, you need to concern yourself not only with food for your body, but with nutrition for your mind and soul.

The thoughts you think, the literature you read, the movies and TV you watch, the people you spend time with, and the people you love all leave a memory that becomes incorporated into your being, either consciously or unconsciously, and becomes part of your new vision of yourself.

You have imagined and visualized the real you. You have imagined and visualized real loving sex. Do not remain disconnected from your destiny any longer. After all, what is a dream without the ability to make it real?

Chapter 5

Exploring Your Body

Now, to begin to understand what your body and mind are capable of, it is necessary to unlock the mystery of sexuality. You have come to understand who you are and who you want to be through visualization, and it is time for the next step, exploring your body.

Stacey and Her Son

Stacey told me about the trip she took with her young son to France. And there, on the chicest and most exclusive beaches, not hidden away, but across from the most expensive hotels on the Riviera, were women alone and with their families, basking in the sun. Walking, sunbathing, chatting.

What astounded Stacey and her son was that most of the women were topless, and nobody thought anything about it. No one stared. It was the natural thing do. And she noticed with surprise that the women did not have young, perfect bodies. They were all ages and all shapes, including fat and droopy. Her son grabbed his camera and pointed it toward a hotel, slyly swiveling back to the beach at the last moment before clicking the shutter.

Stacey wanted to take off her bathing suit top, too, to feel the sun and breeze and freedom. But her son had been brought up in a different culture, and she didn't want to embarrass him. He was shocked by what he saw, and neither he nor his mother discussed the subject. It would have embarrassed him even more.

Just as naked breasts are natural in this French setting, so our attitudes and familiarity with our bodies should be easy, comfortable, and natural. Yet in America many still have lingering inhibitions that are readily communicated as behavioral, if not verbal, messages to our children. For many of my patients, the permission I gave them as their doctor to explore and examine themselves, as I am giving you here, was the first time anyone had said it was okay, much less desirable.

To discover your sexuality as part of becoming a truly liberated, sensual, and loving person, you must explore your body.

When a man touches a woman, her mind and heart can be there, her desire and love, but if she is uncomfortable or ashamed of her body, if she doesn't know it and understand it, the whole experience will be threatened with failure and frustration.

This chapter shows you how to use your senses to get in touch with your physical self. How to understand your sexual body and its delightful secrets. This is crucial to beginning to learn what sexuality is and how to use it to heal problems, pain, depression, and illness so that you bloom and flourish, bursting with good health and joy.

Women vs. Men

Understanding both the differences and similarities between women and men is important. Women and men really are different. Women relate with their heart and soul rather than with their genitals. In this sense they are sexual introverts. Their reproductive organs are internal, protected. Women mentally contain their sexuality and guard it.

Men, on the other hand, are sexual extroverts. Their sexual organs themselves are exposed and their aggressive sexual attitudes are flaunted with pride.

Men's sexual self-image is centered around the hard, aroused, penetrating penis and the explosion of the ejaculation. Men are expected to be knowing about sex, while women are expected to be responsive to that knowing.

This is why men expect loving to manifest itself by immediate genital contact, in direct contrast to women's expectation of being loved by lingering affectionate sensuality, caressing kisses, and gentle touches before genital penetration.

Unfortunately, men know very little and, even worse, seem not to care about learning how to become tuned to what it takes to arouse and satisfy a woman. It's not only the blast of a quick orgasm that he has learned to expect that bothers women, but what really gets to them is that he spends very little time becoming expertly familiar with their erogenous areas and intimate sensuality.

Since sexual communication has been embarrassing and limited from childhood, many women have at one time or another experienced painful sexual relations. That causes them to become apprehensive, passive, uninspired, anorgasmic, or, even to avoid sex. This is somewhat like the child who puts his hand on a hot stove. He's going to avoid it in the future. The answer for the woman, of course, is to know your body, know what hurts and what doesn't, what feels good and what doesn't, and to share that with your partner.

The Case of Carol

Carol, thirty-four, told me how it hurt when her husband attempted sex with her. He didn't take the time to use any lubricant, he didn't spend any time with foreplay. He simply straddled her and thrust himself in, which hurt her. By learning more about her body, Carol was able to let her lover know how to arouse her first so she would feel pleasure and not pain.

Also, many men don't realize the vagina is on an angle toward the small of the back. If the man jams his penis straight in, he may bang into the woman's bladder and cause her pain or contribute to bladder infection. (See Fig. 3.) It is up to the man to ask his partner if anything is uncomfortable and to learn from her answers. It's up to the woman to guide her partner so the loving experience is one of joyful celebration rather than fearful anticipation.

Sexual Abuse

There are women who seem to carry with them a psychological pain in their vaginas as a result of sexual violation, sometimes by a relative, which in my clinical experience occurs far more frequently than one would expect.

In the more than ten thousand women I have seen in my medical practice, I found that a shocking thirty percent believe they have been subjected to an abusive relationship. These figures echo the findings reported in *Sex in America*. It was shown that about twenty percent of women say they have been sexually abused as children and another twenty percent say they have been forced to have sex against their will. Over time, the abused woman may feel so guilty about the sexual activities to which she was subjected (which were clearly either wrong, incestuous, or both) even though she didn't cause them, even though she was the victim, she assumes the responsibility in her subconscious mind and punishes herself and those closest to her.

This woman's vagina reminds her of her guilt and great psychological pain, and she will be unable to have fulfilling sexual relations until she can understand she was not at fault, and come to accept her body in a new way, as belonging totally to her.

A Guide to Self-Exploration

Now, let us begin to explore the female and male bodies, and let's call it **sexploration** to emphasize the lighthearted, fun attitude you need to bring with you.

First, open your heart and see yourself without programming or prejudgment. Do not take yourself too seriously in this exercise. I remember in my youth I was so upset about my difficulty in understanding the problems I was having with my girlfriend that my grandmother, one of the great inspirations in my life, gave me a small plaque that I kept in the kitchen for years. It was of a panda bear upside down, kind of rolling, laughing, and smiling, as panda bears are wont to do. And underneath the panda bear it said, YOU CAN'T TAKE LIFE TOO SERIOUSLY.

So, with a sense of levity and laughter and joyful loving of yourself, begin these exercises I am about to describe. They will eventually lead to bodily pleasure, a delighted heart, and enchantment and magic in your life.

Romantic love provides the emotional food from which sexual energy springs, and the connection of love to another person starts with the connection of love to yourself. **In order to give all of yourself to another person, you must be in possession of that which you give. You must understand your own body.**

The Senses

To begin your exploration, you should fine-tune your sense organs. They are your eyes, nose, ears, tongue, and skin. These organs receive information from your senses which are:

Taste
Sound

Touch
Sight
Smell

Your sense organs communicate this information from the world around you by sending electrical energy through your nervous system to your mind, which perceives what is happening.

The mind takes this information and interprets it. That interpretation depends on the emotional information also being sent from other parts of your brain. For example, if you were being stroked on your arm by your lover, it would feel good. But if your arm were being stroked and you turned and saw that it was not your lover but a lecherous, ugly stranger, it would no longer feel good.

Or, to put it another way, it's like eating chocolate-covered grasshoppers, which were delicious until someone told you what they were.

Your sexual senses are therefore affected by your state of mind.

Now, here are a few ideas to get you started sharpening some of your senses:

Taste

Curl your tongue behind your lower front teeth and suck. With some practice you'll be able to taste the sweet saliva that is contained within the glands under the base of your tongue. It's delightful to bring this saliva into sex play, particularly with kissing or for lubrication. Notice its sweetness. With practice you can get quite a large amount from this location. Notice how good it tastes and think of your lover as you're doing this.

Taste your skin. Lick, nibble, and suck your forearm, hands, fingers, or any accessible part.

If you are curious about what your vagina might taste like, gently place a finger in a moist area near your vaginal opening and taste it. You may be surprised by how natural and unoffensive the experience is.

Sound

Put your head back and place your two fingers in your ears until they are blocked off. Lift your elbows up to the sides and gently vibrate your elbows and arms. If you listen carefully, you will hear the vibration of universal energy that is flowing from the universe into your body through your arms and ears.

This is a very ancient technique but one that reminds us of the tremendous connection we all have, in a vibrational and energetic sense, to our universe. Remove your fingers from your ears.

- Listen to the rhythm of your breathing as you examine yourself.
- Listen to the sound of nature. Birds singing, rain on your window.
- Listen to the sound of music. Discover music you can connect to and which will uplift you. Play it loudly so it throbs inside you.

Touch

Choose your favorite oil. I often recommend buying two or three oils to begin with to see which you prefer. A light sesame body oil is a favorite and is available in most drugstores. You can also use apricot, almond, coconut, olive, sunflower, safflower, or any good massage oil.

Try to give yourself a nonsexual, vigorous massage daily after your morning shower while you are still damp. Rub your body and feet with a small amount of oil. This will enhance your circulation, improve your muscle tone, and detoxify the fat and subcutaneous poisons in your body by gently pushing them away from intercellular spaces under your skin and into the lymphatic vessels, where they are carried to detoxification centers such as the liver, spleen, and kidneys.

Do your neck, breasts, shoulders, chest, abdomen, joints, back, spine, and whatever you can reach. Use a straight motion for the long parts of your body such as your arms and legs and a circular motion over your joints and the rest of your body. Always massage toward the heart.

Sight

Look in your full-length mirror and examine every part of the body you have just oiled. See what makes a woman's body so lovely. The breasts, waist, hips, buttocks, toes. See what makes a man's body so lovely. The arm muscles, broad chest, firm thighs. Look and enjoy what you see.

It's yours.

Smell

Take this opportunity to smell your body, your skin, under your arms, your hair if it is long, touch and smell your vagina or the hair around your penis and testicles.

Now that you have begun to connect with your senses of taste, sound, touch, sight and smell, it's time to take a longer, deeper look at your sexual self.

Stay with Yourself

Plan time to be with yourself. Turn off the phone, faxes, close and lock the door. Plan to be with yourself for at least an hour, or even two, without interruption. Think about the things you want in your environment when your begin to explore yourself. You need a bedroom that is secure and private.

Lie in bed.

Relax.

Using your newly sharpened sense of touch, gently caress your entire body.

Explore the sensation with both your hands using your fingertips, your palms, or even the backs of your hands. As a surgeon, I know your fingertips are the most sensitive part of your hand. Use clippers and a nail file regularly. Long nails tend to interfere with the sensitivity of your fingertips and certainly will interfere with uninhibited vaginal, penile, and anal (yes, this too) exploration.

Explore different kinds of touch and how they feel: squeezing, kneading, scratching, tapping, slapping, brushing. Vary the speed and pressure.

Explore your entire body.

Touches are very similar to kisses with your fingers and hands.

Be conscious of your own touch and the way it feels.

An erotic touch requires a receptiveness to sexual energy, whether it comes from yourself or your partner.

Explore your hair, your scalp, your brow, your face, your nose, your eyes, your ears, your earlobes, your neck, your armpits, your stomach, your belly button, the lips around your vagina or your testicles. Notice your legs, back, buttocks, anus, and all parts of you. This is the body you have to work with now.

It is absolutely essential that you love and accept your body so that you can be sexually loving with it.

This is not to say that everyone can't be a little thinner or a little stronger or a little bigger or smaller. But at the moment this is how you are and this is how you must accept yourself to be healthy in your love of yourself.

Try to obtain a standing floor mirror that swivels, the kind Grandma used to have. They can be found in most furniture stores.

You will also need a broad-based standing flashlight, or a standing lighted makeup mirror.

Anatomy 101 for Men and Women

Now prepare to examine your body more closely than you have ever done before. Understanding your own genital exploration will be much easier if you know a little basic anatomy and some general principles of human development.

Rather than using oversimplified schematic line drawings, through the courtesy of Novartis Pharmaceuticals Corporation, the drawings of Frank Netter, M.D., medicine's Michelangelo, are being reproduced here for your current and future reference.

I have chosen these drawings not only because they are clear, detailed, and the finest art in medicine, but because they are the very same illustrations that helped me understand anatomy when I was in medical school. You will find yourself referring to them time after time, and the information you can learn by studying them as you explore yourself and your partner is endless. You will be able to identify your different body parts, see where they are and how they connect to one another. You will also be able to compare men's and women's anatomy.

I have left many structures identified that will not be mentioned here, or are academic and primarily of interest to doctors. This was done intentionally so that in the future you may refer to these accurate renderings of your reproductive anatomy for additional information.

Figure 1 shows corresponding parts of the male and female external genital organs. Structures that are the same color come from the same area in the embryo. All babies, when they first start to grow as a fertilized egg until they are five or six weeks old, are undifferentiated embryos—that is, the physical gender differences do not show despite being predetermined at the time of fertilization by the chromosomes, (xx=female; xy=male).

Notice the following similarities in the adult male and female:

> head of male penis=head of female clitoris (yellow in both sexes)
> shaft of penis=shaft of clitoris (blue in both sexes)
> penoscrotal raphe under penis=labium minus (pink in both sexes)
> scrotum=labium majus (purple in both sexes)

Homologies of Male and Female Genitalia

The genitalia of both sexes arise from common sites in the human embryo.
same color = same site of origin

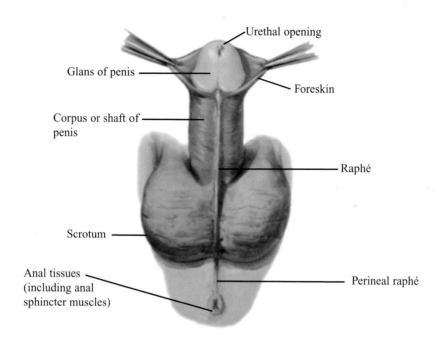

Urethal opening

Glans of penis

Foreskin

Corpus or shaft of penis

Raphé

Scrotum

Anal tissues (including anal sphincter muscles)

Perineal raphé

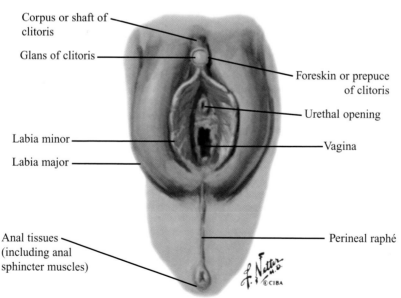

Corpus or shaft of clitoris

Glans of clitoris

Foreskin or prepuce of clitoris

Urethal opening

Labia minor

Vagina

Labia major

Anal tissues (including anal sphincter muscles)

Perineal raphé

Female Genital Organs

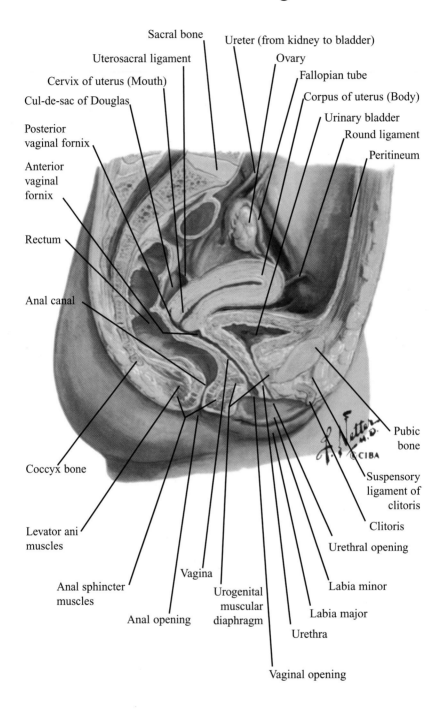

Sacral bone

Ureter (from kidney to bladder)

Uterosacral ligament

Ovary

Cervix of uterus (Mouth)

Fallopian tube

Cul-de-sac of Douglas

Corpus of uterus (Body)

Posterior vaginal fornix

Urinary bladder

Round ligament

Anterior vaginal fornix

Peritineum

Rectum

Anal canal

Pubic bone

Coccyx bone

Suspensory ligament of clitoris

Levator ani muscles

Clitoris

Urethral opening

Vagina

Anal sphincter muscles

Labia minor

Anal opening

Urogenital muscular diaphragm

Labia major

Urethra

Vaginal opening

Female External Genital Organs

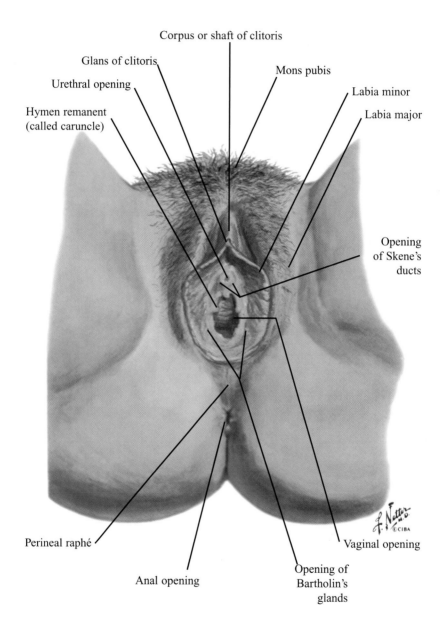

Corpus or shaft of clitoris

Glans of clitoris

Mons pubis

Urethral opening

Labia minor

Hymen remanent
(called caruncle)

Labia major

Opening
of Skene's
ducts

Perineal raphé

Vaginal opening

Anal opening

Opening of
Bartholin's
glands

Male Genital Organs

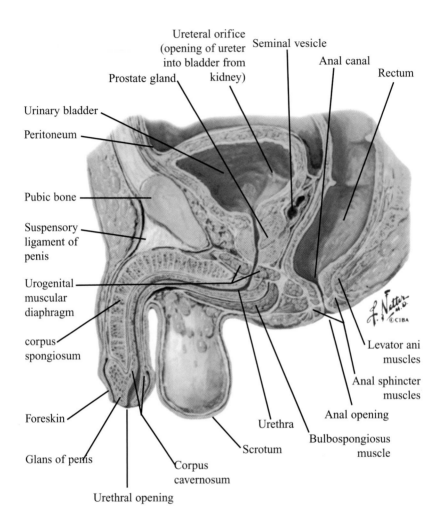

Ureteral orifice (opening of ureter into bladder from kidney)

Seminal vesicle

Anal canal

Rectum

Prostate gland

Urinary bladder

Peritoneum

Pubic bone

Suspensory ligament of penis

Urogenital muscular diaphragm

corpus spongiosum

Foreskin

Glans of penis

Urethral opening

Corpus cavernosum

Scrotum

Urethra

Levator ani muscles

Anal sphincter muscles

Anal opening

Bulbospongiosus muscle

f. Netter M.D. ©CIBA

line behind genitals and before anus=perineal raphe (pink both sexes)

perianal tissue=perianal tissue (pink both sexes)

This helps to understand why these areas feel alike when touched, caressed, stroked, licked, or physically loved. As a matter of fact, the same type of sucking that men call "blow jobs" or "giving head" works on the women's corresponding part, the clitoris. In this sense we are more similar than many would like to acknowledge.

Figure 2 and **Figure 3** show the female outside and inside. Figure 2 is a very clear, accurate image of what you will see when you explore yourself visually with a mirror, as described later in this chapter.

Figure 3 demonstrates among other things the presence of the urethral opening at the vaginal entry and the angle of the vagina toward the small of the back. Note the most comfortable position for tampon insertion as well as penetration of the penis is following this angle. Notice that straight-in penetration may bump a full bladder. (This is what causes "honeymoon cystitis.")

The **cervix** protrudes into the top of the vagina, and you may feel this during self-exploration. Notice the opening in the middle. Note it is connected to the body of the uterus, which in turn connects higher up inside to the fallopian tubes and ovaries. This is why deep penetration where the penis bumps the cervix may hurt, because it shakes the uterus, which jars the tubes and ovaries. Discomfort also occurs if you have a cyst of the ovary or inflammation of the uterus or tubes.

The **G-spot** is on the front wall of the vagina (in front of the cervix, behind the bladder) and between the line labeled "anterior vaginal fornix" and the line labeled "vagina." Note that you must curl your fingers forward toward the belly button to reach this area. Also note that the lower rectum comes very close to this area. This is why some women feel they have better access to their G-spot from an anal approach.

The **anus** leads into the rectum, which, when empty, has plenty of room to accommodate a penis provided insertion is slow, lubricated, and gentle, the external anal sphincter muscle is relaxed, and the man is not simply too large to get past the sphincter.

The uterosacral ligament goes from the uterus to the lower back. It contains many nerves and is why women have backaches with some uterine medical problems (menstrual periods, uterine infections, endometriosis). The rectouterine pouch (cul-de-sac of Douglas) is on top of the vagina on the abdominal side. Just above it is the end of the fallopian tubes. If, during menstruation, lining tissue from inside the uterus is forced to drip backward out of the straw-like tubes (for example if the cervical opening is too small and creates an obstruction to the free flow of menstrual blood and tissue), then the tissue may drop here, start to grow, and bleed monthly, just as if it were still inside the uterus. This condition, called endometriosis, is very common. It is why women with this disorder frequently have painful intercourse with deep penetration but not with insertion.

The **uterus** is on top of the bladder. If it enlarges with fibroids or other growths, or when it drops into the stretched vagina following childbirth, it may put external pressure on the bladder causing frequent urination.

Figure 4, the male figure, is complicated but has a great deal of information. Note the corpus cavernosum and the corpus spongiosum of the penis. These are the spongelike structures that fill with blood and cause an erection. Note the long distance from the tip of the penis to the urinary bladder. This is why men get fewer bladder infections than women. Note, too, the long distance sperm must travel in the vas deferens from the testicles through the prostate (where seminal fluid is produced) and down and out of the penis.

The **vas deferens** is what is cut and tied in a vasectomy for male sterilization. The prostate and seminal vesicles contain the fluid that mixes with the sperm from the testicles to produce an ejaculation.

The **prostate** is in back of the bladder (thus men with prostate enlargement have difficulty starting urination, or slow or sputtering urinary streams) and in front of the rectum (and so is accessible for medical examination or playful exploration through the anus).

Many other aspects of these detailed illustrations will be referred to in subsequent chapters. Look at them as often as necessary to understand the body's anatomy, your body, and your lover's body.

Now let us turn from illustrations to the real thing.

Chapter 6

The Essential Body
and Its Orgasm

You can't understand your sexuality without first knowing yourself. So, here goes, first for women and then for men. You will need your freestanding lighted makeup mirror, your standing full-length mirror, a flashlight, and perhaps a lubricant such as Astroglide. Although you can do only what is suggested for your own gender, it will be useful to read both sections.

Exploration for Women

Take your lighted magnifying makeup mirror and while standing, look at the area between your legs. Compare it to Figure 2.

That *entire* area between your legs is known as the vulva, not the vagina, as people mistakenly call it. The vagina is an internal organ. The vulva is external.

Examine your pubic hair, and if it is more than approximately a half inch long, trim it with a small scissors, since excessive hair on the pubic-vulval-anal area can absorb a lot of lubricant, whether natural or from a tube, and get sticky and messy.

Now place the mirror on the floor and squat down over it. It is time to see yourself as you never have seen yourself before. Refer to Figure 2 as you carefully examine your external genital organs.

Ideally, if you would like to see what you look like inside, don't feel embarrassed to discuss it with your gynecologist. Gynecologists are very responsive to patients who want to learn more about their bodies. It's healthy to ask. "I'm curious to see what I look like inside. Could you help me to look with a mirror while you're examining me?"

But for now, take two fingers, one from each hand, and spread your vaginal lips. You will notice that the hair-bearing area changes in color to a wet, glistening pink. If exposed to a lot of soap and water over the years, this tissue, called the vaginal mucosa, will dry out and wrinkle just as the bottoms of your feet do when you stay in the bath too long. This is the result of overzealous cleansing and is clearly not something a woman would want.

Notice your clitoris, its shaft and tip. As I explained, the clitoris is embryologically just like the male penis. And the sensations from the head and shaft of the clitoris are similar to what a man feels in the same areas. Also, the same nerves that enervate the clitoris, vulva, and testicles also enervate the anal areas, so the orgasmic potential there is virtually equal.

Now look back a little bit and you will notice the opening of the urethra. This is the exit for urine. Because of the short distance between the vaginal opening of the urethra and the bladder (less than two inches), a woman is exposed to bladder infections if this area is not kept clean. It is important, therefore, to urinate and empty the bladder before and after sex play to flush the bacteria that may have swum into the urethra.

Some women find the urethra and the area in front of it very sensitive. These should be gently touched and explored.

Notice the hymen or the remnants of where the hymen used to be. (See the hymenal caruncle, Fig. 2.) It separates the inner vagina from the outer vagina. This is important because the outer vagina responds to different hormones than the inner vagina. While this is not particularly relevant to young women in the reproductive years, it is especially important in the menopausal years, when sex hormones are low and the vulva may be dry and has shrunk.

Now, squatting over your lighted mirror, put two lubricated fingers in your vagina. The index and third are easiest. Notice the horizontal ridges on the walls. The more ridges there are, the more glistening and moist, the more estrogen hormone there is in your body.

Next, explore inside while you bend your fingers forward toward your pubic bone and belly button. (Follow Fig. 3 to know what you are touching.) You will feel the urethra opening, and as you slide in you will feel where the urethra connects to the base of the bladder.

Moving deeper still toward your front with your fingers together, you will cross the area known as the G-spot. This is not a specific spot but a confluence of nerves, which, during arousal, are particularly sensitive in most women.

Farther up and back, remembering the angle of the vagina is toward the small of the back, you will notice the cervix. It feels like the tip of your nose. It is firm and has a small crater in the middle, which is the cervical opening.

If you move the cervix a little, since it's attached to the uterus, like the elbow to the arm, you will be wiggling the uterus. Significant tenderness from this motion should remind you that this area can be rather vigorously pounded during aggressive and enthusiastic sexual intercourse, a situation that should cause you to alter positions or, if still painful, consult a doctor.

You will not be able to feel the ovaries or the uterus with self-exploration.

Moving farther back, some women can push way in and feel their spine, an area which the baby's head must pass through. Pushing as deep as your fingers will reach, and down toward the rectum, you may feel the end of your tailbone (the coccyx) with your fingertips.

There is a hammocklike group of muscles of substantial strength in both sexes that start at the pubic bone (in front of the vagina or scrotum) and extend around the rectum to the base of the spine.

This muscular sling occupies the pelvic floor and in women acts like a cradle for their sexual organs.

These muscles contract and relax during sex and go into spasms of contraction during orgasm. Part of the group is the frequently mentioned PC muscle, which is short for pubococcygeas. This goes from the pubic bone to the coccyx, or tailbone.

I call all the muscles in this area, which are used in the process of loving, the Love Muscles. What they are and how to strengthen them will be discussed further in Chapter 16.

Before finishing your exploration, a woman may again look in the standing long floor mirror, appreciate the beauty of her body, its contours, shapes, and remember the hormone-induced physical changes that occur with menstruation. There is a fullness and slight tenderness of the breasts, a slight swelling of the abdomen from water retention and gas accumulating from the slowing down of food passing through the intestines as a result of increased progesterone, and a swelling of the brain from water retention, which puts pressure on the brain and sometimes results in irritability or headaches, also due to hormones.

Your men say, "Oh, you are so irritable, you must be getting your period." Well, this is why. They would too if their bodies changed so dramatically. Remind yourself that no matter what time of month it is, you're still beautiful. Regular slightly crampy periods with associated premenstrual breast tenderness and moodiness are a sign of ovulation and, thus, fertility.

Mapping the Woman's Erogenous Zones

Having explored your body you are ready to begin stimulating yourself sexually. This is called **masturbation** and is best done lying down in bed. It is a completely natural and healthy way to relieve sexual tension. As you play with your vulva or penis and entire genital area, you will make your body feel good all over.

This exercise will teach you things about where you feel especially arousable. I suggest that you map out mentally where the sensations of your body are most exciting. Learn what touch most pleases, and what tempo is most stimulating. This requires that you repeat the exercise a number of times; it is not meant to be a one-time experience.

You can use this information to teach your lover where, when, and how you become really excited. Or use it to stimulate yourself if you find yourself alone one day. Or if you are single and want an exciting sex life, do it to ensure your own mental and physical health. Remember that almost any area of your body can be an erogenous zone. The most common ones are:

- Behind the ears
- The line from front to back under the tongue and behind the upper lip
- the underarms
- the nipples
- the sides of the breasts
- the lower abdomen
- the pubic area
- the vulva and pelvic area
- the buttocks
- the anus and the area around it
- the inner thighs
- behind the knees, particularly when the legs are slightly bent
- the feet and toes

Notice how good it feels to have a delicate touch behind your ear. Notice how nice patting feels on your tummy, on your buttocks. Or how good stroking on your inner thighs, lower abdomen, or clitoris feels.

Put your lubricated fingers on the clitoris and notice which areas change on arousal and how different areas become more sensitive.

Explore yourself sensually.

Dwell on those areas that feel the best and allow yourself to become stimulated.

Fantasize as freely as you like.

Continue the stimulation until you are almost at orgasm. For many women this is best done on your stomach with the legs slightly spread. For others it is best done on your back with your hips on a pillow and the legs up or down.

Keep track of the areas that are aroused on the outside of your body as well as the inside.

Add to your mental map as you make these new explorations.

Experiment with different locations and intensities and different types of movement.

Build a library of erotic images or scenes you can think about that turn you on.

As a child delights in exploring the unknown, remember those areas that work best for you, bearing in mind that these may change with more experience, as you find variety more pleasurable.

Reaching the point of orgasm requires complete self-confidence in the safety, security, and privacy of where you are, as well as comfort with your body. **What is essential is that you must have the willful, conscious intention to let go. JUST LET GO.**

Exploration for Men

For the man to begin to understand his own sexuality, he needs to make perhaps a greater psychological leap than a woman does.

Men expect, and are expected, to know everything about sex without any education.

What they have learned usually comes from inept initial experiences modified by locker-room banter. Men take pride in their masculinity and most suppress any opportunity to seek out legitimate sources of information. Often, what is reinforced is the gunslinger attitude, counting each conquest as a notch on a gun handle. It's obvious that this traps most men in perpetual ignorance.

Too often you focus on the immediate objective of your rigid penis and the explosion of ejaculation.

You the powerful conquerer. You Tarzan.

She the submissive receptacle. She helpless Jane.

Men need to move from a penis and orgasm focus (the "I want to get laid" attitude) to a caring, loving, whole-body responsiveness where they are able to give as well as receive nongenital loving affection. I repeat—nongenital.

It means acknowledging and going beyond the slam-bam-thank-you-ma'am mentality. If you get to know your lover's body as well as your own, you will see all the nonorgasmic delights available by using your senses to touch and feel her, to smell and hear her. To watch her. To taste her. To truly love her.

It makes sense to use your senses, all of them.

Mapping the Man's Erogenous Zones

When it comes to enjoying their own nonorgasmic delights, few men are aware, for example, of the tremendous pleasure to be derived from stimulation of the line between the back of the testicles and the front of the anus.

And even fewer men are aware of the intense erotic pleasure to be derived from the massage and stimulation of the prostate gland through the rectum.

So it is that you need to increase your body awareness with exploration as much as a woman. Not only to be able to ejaculate (most men have masturbated) but also to enhance your awareness of the pleasures to be derived from the nonrigid penis, orgasm without ejaculation, and from enjoying all of your erogenous zones with all of your senses.

You will need to be willing and motivated to expand your sexual horizons.

Most men think they know it all.
But do you really?

You won't get there watching Sunday afternoon football. You have to actively commit to learning how to be sensual and sexually decentered rather than always having your eye on penetration and orgasm. Men must learn this just as much as women must learn to be more sexually aggressive and more genitally focused.

You will need to start by bringing into your mind an awareness of the sexual potential of all your senses.

A good way to start is sight.

You should look at yourself in the full-length mirror, seeing your body and accepting it, just as women must. Accept the fact that you may have love handles, or you may be overweight, or too short or too tall, or balding, or your penis may be too short or too large or in some way imperfect.

Remember, this is the body you should love, the temple of your mind and spirit.

I recommend the same bathing as I urged for women, and a massage with a light sesame oil found in pharmacies. Skip the deodorants during your exploration or sex play, since the pheromones, or sexual hormones, produced in the genital and underarm areas are especially arousing to the subconscious mind.

Having explored yourself thoroughly in an entirely nonerotic fashion, envision yourself now in an erotic situation (fantasy) and massage yourself all over with kneading, squeezing, pinching, scratching, tapping, stroking movements of your fingertips, the base of your fingers, you whole hand and the back of your hand. Include your:

- scalp
- ears
- underarms
- abdomen
- back
- penis

- anus
- testicles
- buttocks
- legs behind the knees
- knees
- feet

As you have seen by examining the illustrations in Chapter 5, male and female genital areas are startlingly equivalent. For example, the hair-bearing scrotum of the man is equivalent to the hair-bearing lips of the woman's vulva.

Now feel the area of your testicles and penis very carefully, and lovingly, then the anus and the anal area. In order to understand this area, after you have had a bowel movement, you should feel the small doughnut-like external anal sphincter and the intense stimulation coming from the tremendous concentration of sensory nerves in this area.

Then take your finger coated in a thick lubricant like Vaseline (you may wish to use a latex glove), place it on the tight doughnut-like sphincter muscle and apply gentle, firm, continuous pressure. Wait until the muscle relaxes and then gently slip it into the anus. Feel what happens when you squeeze your sphincter around your fingertip several times. This is what happens during orgasm. Now, seated on the toilet or in bed with your legs up, reach in, flexing your finger forward toward your belly button in a come-hither motion to find the prostate gland.

The prostate feels walnut-sized and is located in the direction of your navel (See Fig. 4). It can be soft and spongy but if you feel it when you are aroused, it becomes engorged with blood, hard and pulsating. During ejaculation it will throb and spasm, since Love Muscles around it squeeze most of the fluid that makes up your ejaculate.

The nerves surrounding the prostate are extremely sensitive to pleasurable stimulation when you are aroused.

But if you don't try it, you won't know.

In my opinion, prostatic massage reduces the risk of prostatic cancer as well as benign prostatic hypertrophy (abnormal enlargement) by increasing the blood circulation.

Knowing and accepting your body and your partner's body, you should be able to have a healthy sex life, communicate with a new openness about your expanded sensuality, and enjoy greater pleasure in the ever-increasing inventory of sexual activity, which will delight your mind and titillate your body.

Medical Advantages of Orgasm

Medically speaking, orgasm has tremendous benefits for women and men.

It causes the release of numerous sex hormones and endorphins that stimulate the body's vital organs and glands, and gives a sense of relief and joy.

It causes a rapid heartbeat and is an excellent form of aerobic exercise.

It creates a detoxification of your entire system as muscles contract in a spasmodic response like a mini-seizure, squeezing toxins and the waste products of metabolism out of the muscles and tissues under the skin.

In fact, the French sometimes call an orgasm *la petite mort,* the "little death," because it is similar to a seizure in the sense that one may lose awareness of time, place, and person in orgasmic ecstasy.

It should be noted that women are capable of having an orgasm from:

> fantasy alone (on rare occasions)
> nipple stimulation alone
> vaginal stimulation alone
> clitoral stimulation alone
> vulval stimulation alone
> anal stimulation alone

It is quite clear that the process from arousal to orgasm is a process that occurs in our minds. The messages go from body to brain, back and forth with ever-increasing intensity. Our mind and emotions together receive and interpret the erotic sensations we feel.

What Is an Orgasm?

The orgasm is a lightning burst of electrical energy surging from the fantasy centers of the brain, speeding through the spinal cord into every nerve, every muscle, every cell of our body. The focus of this energy is on erogenous areas, particularly the nipples and clitoris, the lower third of the vagina, where the Love Muscles are, the anus, and the penis.

What happens is this:

Sexual stimulation affects the whole body as excitement builds, respiration increases, heart rate increases, blood pressure rises. Blood vessel congestion occurs in the skin, causing flushing, perspiration, and an increased feeling of warmth. Muscles become tense, and just before orgasm the toes may flex.

With women the first general response to sexual excitement is the lubrication of the vagina through the vaginal walls. As filling up of the blood vessels continues, the vaginal walls thicken and grow dark. The inner two thirds of the vagina expand and lengthen, creating an empty space, and the outer third and labia swell and darken.

In men the penis becomes even more erect, and the glans, or head of the penis, becomes enlarged and takes on a purple hue. The testicles also become enlarged fifty to one hundred percent and become elevated against the body cavity. The scrotum is drawn up. Tiny glands secrete a small amount of clear fluid that appears at the opening of the penis. This is sweet and unrelated to ejaculation. The prostate gland expands in size and becomes firm and easy to feel.

In both sexes, the hands and legs become rigid and extended, facial muscles become contorted, nipples become erect. The person seems to be gasping for breath and may moan or scream.

In men the orgasm begins with the ejaculations of the vas deferens, the seminal vesicles, and prostate gland. These organs pour their contents into the ejaculatory duct. And this movement of fluid feels like "I'm about to come."

In the second stage of the man's orgasm, powerful contractions spread through the prostate gland and the Love Muscles around the penis and urethra propelling semen out.

The woman who can masturbate herself to a climax may enjoy seeing what is happening to her body. Watch yourself in front of your lighted makeup mirror so you can see the swelling of your labia and the beautiful color changes from pale pink to bright pink to bright red and purple that occur during arousal.

Note the clear fluid produced just before you come. Also notice the beautiful spasms of the Love Muscles around your vaginal opening and anus. This is what your man would see if he could watch you. And most men would like to.

By exploring yourself frequently, you will become aware of your body's erotic map and be able to communicate not only with your partner but with yourself, enjoying ever-increasing and expanding sensual activities that will delight your mind and inspire your spirit.

There is another advantage to being familiar with the body you live in. Through exploration you not only enhance your ability to experience sexual pleasure but increase your awareness of internal signals warning you of unhealthy bodily changes. **Your body speaks to you if you listen.**

Listening to Body Signals

Wendy was very worried about breast cancer because her mother had it. She checked her breasts but she never really checked them well because she was afraid she might feel something abnormal and not know how to interpret it.

Nevertheless, she became familiar with her breasts, noting how they felt at different times of her cycle. She noticed they were softer after her periods and became lumpier and more tender just before her periods, when they felt almost like beanbags, mostly in the upper outer quarter. Her nipples also became slightly tender.

She shared this fear with her partner. She explained there was no particular lump that stood out above the others, as bigger or harder, but there was this general lumpiness that subsided with the onset of her period.

When she spoke to me and described her symptoms, she discovered she had virtually made the diagnosis herself of mild fibrocystic disease, a benign disorder that affects one out of every two women and is characterized by small cysts forming in the milk glands due to the rise and fall of the hormone estrogen.

These cysts increase in size at the end of the menstrual cycle and cause local irritation that results in fibrous tissue being laid down to isolate and protect the rest of the breast from the small cysts. It's like a callous protecting your foot from a poorly fitting shoe. This creates the tender lumpiness, which, over time, results in grisly lumpy areas of the breast that may be difficult to distinguish from breast cancer.

I advised her to reduce her dietary intake of methylxanthines by eliminating foods that contain them, coffee, tea, cola drinks, chocolate, and nuts, because they are known to stimulate the development of fibrocystic disease. I also suggested she reduce vigorous sexual fondling of her breasts during this time of her cycle. I recommended 1,000 IU of vitamin E a day in order to inhibit cyst formation in her breasts, and told her to wear a supportive bra at all times. She was to report any lump that stood out from the others.

Since historically more than fifty percent of all breast cancers are diagnosed by self-examination, coming to know her body well led Wendy not only to a complete and healing sexuality, which she vigorously enjoyed, but a clear understanding of a minor health problem that she was able to self-monitor for the rest of her life.

For men there are also medical advantages to knowing your body. Ann and her husband, Charlie, came to see me on an emergency visit one June afternoon. It seems that during lovemaking the night before, she had been sucking her husband's testicles, when she had been shocked to notice a hard lump on the left one.

She mentioned it to Charlie, but he was too engrossed to stop and pay attention. However, the next morning he came out of the shower pale and obviously frightened. Ann asked him if he had felt it too. He said that at thirty-three years old, he was sure it couldn't be serious, but yes, he had.

Since he didn't have his own doctor or medical plan because he was self-employed and had never been sick enough to need one, Ann brought him to see me. Just as they feared, when I examined him, there was a solid hard lump in his left testicle. This later turned out to be testicular cancer.

It was a good moral for me that I pass on to you.

Check your testicles once a month just like women check their breasts.

As you can see, if you increase your awareness through exploration of your body and your sexuality, you not only enhance your ability to perceive sexual pleasure, you become aware of what your body is like during different stages of arousal, and in different circumstances, and you will be better able to check for early signs of disease.

How great it is that you can know the map that takes you to all the secret places and all the sensitive nooks, folds, protrusions, creases, crevices, cracks, crannies, and openings of the body that belongs only to you.

Chapter 7

The Beauty
of Love

We should love as we wish to be loved, sexually and otherwise.

You can have sex with a stranger, even great sex, but you cannot love someone you do not know and share life with.

Sex without mind or emotion is disconnected, isolating, and ultimately destructive to self-respect and mental and spiritual health. But sexuality drawn from the energetic source of existence in mind and soul connects our highest values and ideals and our most beautiful and fulfilling actions.

There isn't a human being alive who doesn't have emotions and doesn't have a subconscious mind in addition to a conscious one, who doesn't have a connection to the universe, perhaps conceived of as God, that is noncognitive, that just exists. That is spiritual.

We all have a mind that is aware of the environment around us, and that mind makes choices on the basis of our values. One thing is more important than another thing. That's what a value is. Therefore we are able to say some things are good, some are bad, and some are better.

So it is that we all have the potential to put our hearts and minds, our spirits and our values, into living love. And living love as sex.

That's all it takes. A receptive, open mind, a willingness to learn about the beauty of love, a heart that gives you spiritual energy to persevere, and a body that is capable.

The sexual energy of love is the drive that takes us closest to the sublime and is the source of creativity, mentally and spiritually.

So, if you are fortunate enough to be with someone you love, share as much of yourself as you can. It is the accumulated history we actively share that bonds us through difficult times of stress, illness, and economic problems. But a shared history with a lover won't necessarily keep the fires roaring, the passions surging, and the hormones raging. A loving sexuality will.

The next chapters show you how to build bonds of love that will weather the storms of life. It is my prescription for you, especially those who have lost yourselves in over zealous commitment to work or in boredom with your partner. More and more staleness creeps into relationships that were once fresh and seemingly perfect. I will describe how to counteract this as I explain how to make love great.

Harry and Louise

Louise spoke to me about the sexual problems she and her husband, Harry, were having. I asked to see Harry alone to get his side of it. I knew he would not talk honestly in her presence. I think many of you will find his problem not unlike your own.

"When you get married you build the person up to be the most perfect person in the world, and that's why you marry her even though she may not be the most beautiful or the smartest. You make her believe she is. At the beginning we had a good sex life.

"But I quickly learned, as time went on, that communication about sex is very hard for people. We can't even communicate about simple things like whether I get to watch the TV show I want.

"I would rather compromise than create conflict. So I watch her show or we sit in separate rooms in front of separate TV sets. The same goes for bringing up anything that bothers me, especially something as touchy as our sex life.

"Our sex gets boring. It is just boring doing the same thing with the same person. Just because we're married doesn't mean that our sex is going to always be great. And people's needs change over the years. I might decide I want to try something different and I know she doesn't. But we can't talk about it because I don't want to hurt her feelings. I can't tell her sex is not exciting anymore, because she will hear that *she* is not exciting anymore.

"I can't explain that letting our sex go downhill is a bad thing to do, but she is not a bad person for doing it.

"I think most men, though, just want to have sex and go to sleep. All the massages, sweet-talk, and foreplay is work. I get home and I'm tired. So we have to compromise again. But I really feel if there is going to be anything new in our sex life, my wife would have to suggest it. It's her responsibility. I don't need it.

"I don't want to be crude, doctor, but no matter what I do, I'm still going to be in bed with the same woman. You can repaint your Ford, but it still won't drive like a Porsche.

"Anyway, I don't think most men talk about sex with their women. Certainly not the ones I know. There is more chance a man will experiment with sexual things with someone he doesn't know than with his wife."

And here is exactly the problem. This man chose to continue with a boring sex life rather than talk to his wife in a way that would not hurt. They couldn't decide together to take the time to try new ways of loving because they never really connected in the first place. **If this sounds like your relationship, don't despair. If you truly want to change to a more fulfilling and loving life, the answers are all contained in the pages that follow.**

Harry and Louise are probably typical of what is going on in many American bedrooms. In the survey *Sex in America,* many couples appear to be disinterested. Even in moments of sexual activity, they are often isolated from the persons with whom they are being intimate. Sex is squirreled away in the latest hours of the evening, in darkened bedrooms, done quickly by tired adults who seek a few spasms of pleasure before sleeping. This sex is not a union of mind, body, and spirit; it is often the briefest of unfulfilled groping by exhausted and uninspired participants.

In fact, the survey found that one third of Americans have sex with their partners only a few times a year or not at all, and only eight percent had sex four or more times a week. And among those who had sex with their partner, how good was it? It was obviously better for men than for women. Seventy-five percent of men reported they always had an orgasm, while only twenty-nine percent of women said they always did. That leaves a shocking seventy-one percent of women who didn't always have an orgasm.

I conclude that most American couples need to work together to overcome fear, embarrassment, and inhibitions. Loving should be a relaxed, playful state of enjoyment. How cruel it would be, in our short lifetimes, to ignore and give up this basic pleasure, which is free to us all. Overcoming impediments to the joy of loving requires a commitment to private time and shared imagination. The rewards in pleasure and improved mental and physical health are overwhelming.

Talking of Love

What a celebration life is when shared with your own committed partner. Sexual loving ennobles mankind and creates a health-promoting happiness that permeates heart and soul. Communication without embarrassment is key.

Lovers communicate via talking, kisses, touches, and movement with sighs and cries, whispers and moans, and verbal expressions. Every lover's sounds are different, and couples must listen carefully to each other to determine the meaning of the sounds.

Couples like Harry and Louise are usually too shy to speak about their preferences. This may be more true of women than of men. A certain degree of shyness is understandable. However, embarrassment in the context of a loving relationship is something that should be overcome.

It is important for you to learn to talk intimately with your partner in order to describe what feels good when you make love and what doesn't.

Of course a woman might not want to say "Listen, I'd really like to have you move your finger in the first inch of my vagina in a forward direction slowly and then hard." For some, it's not only difficult to tell your lover what to do, you probably won't find it comfortable to say the words "vagina" or "penis" out loud. It's easier for a woman to communicate what she wants her lover to do by putting her hand down and gently showing him what she likes.

But when one tells the other what they want, it is extremely important to use only **positive** communication. As in the visualization exercise in Chapter 4, always try to be positive (unless, of course, pain short-circuits communication pleasantries).

Never say "Don't do that."

Or "I don't like that. Stop it!"

Or "Quit it!"

Do say "I like it so much better when you do this."

Or "Darling, pressing lightly really turns me on."

Or "Honey, I really love it when you move a little bit forward and a little faster."

Words that are negative communications tend to be closing, discouraging, and limiting toward present and future understanding.

Words that are positive communications are positively received and encouraging.

Remember, communication is built on a groundwork of trust and that trust is built on shared knowledge and experience. So, with your lover, always express what you like approvingly and lovingly. And *listen* to what your lover communicates.

For some of you who are more emotional and less verbal, words can often sound too clinical and technical. Then be emotional and act out what you want to say. As long as you communicate. That is the important thing. If you find it easier to explain your sexual preferences while responding to what you like with your own sounds of pleasure, do that.

Sounds of love should be practiced. Many of us don't have the privacy or opportunity to be loud lovers, but revealing what you want is incomplete without sound. Practice making any sound while exhaling when loving.

Learn to express sounds and words of love that communicate levels of arousal, to express your growing emotion, the drawing near of your orgasm. Make the sound louder and longer the more aroused you are or change it in pitch or quality.

Learn to express praise and joy at what feels good.

You'll soon condition your lover to respond with delight to the sound or word signals you are giving him or her.

Many people are uncomfortable expressing sounds or talking during lovemaking. However, it is important to get over that and to express pleasure and degrees of elation. While many conjure up a fantasy in their minds to arouse themselves to the point of orgasm, a more sophisticated, conscious way of using the mind is to communicate by sound and deed so effectively that the sexual act itself is elevated to a fantasy that sparks orgasm. This is why eye contact during the act of loving is so important.

Advanced Lovemaking

In loving, the ideas are not consciously processed first by the analytical mind. For example, you don't stop to think "Shall I move this way or that? Faster or slower? What is he thinking? Will she like this?" With skilled lovers, loving just flows.

Your thinking, your movements, your emotion, come directly from the heart. The woman becomes beautiful, the man tells her of her beauty and importance to him, how he values her, how deeply he loves her, and how much he is becoming part of her and she part of him. She is empowered by these words and uplifted to a state of joy, respect, love, and ecstasy. It is the sweetest gift he can give her.

This is beyond the first level of lovemaking. I call it Advanced Lovemaking. Fantasy has now become irrelevant because you are beyond fantasy. You are in a world where eroticism is an incomparable peak that you are scaling easily in the moments leading to orgasm. Fantasy is unimportant because you are living, breathing, and feeling a flawless truth. An emotional peak that is pure, beautiful, and supremely erotic. You have arrived at a point beyond fantasy, a true celebration of your nature and love.

To get there, you have stretched your boundaries, explored yourself, your contradictions, and your perceived limits. You have decided to refuse to get stuck in fixed sexual roles or rigid sexual concepts that confine and constrain you. As men and women, you appreciate that it is our differences that keep us endlessly fascinated. With delight, whimsy, and humor your freed imagination and creativity as lovers now takes you to intimate places where the mundane gives way to the sublime.

The spiritual, physical, and mental climax in the dance of love is, of course, the orgasm. This explosion of ecstatic feeling for both men and women can be a cosmic experience. It is the ultimate expansion of one's self into and beyond the realm of physical reality. For a few precious moments, you have left earth and are soaring through the heavens.

Chapter 8

Preparing
for Lovemaking

While society and the media may hype the idea of raw sex, instant gratification, and impulsive satisfaction, the truth is that although spontaneous sex can be great, great sex is worthy of planning and ritual. Think of it as an important banquet for very important guests. You wouldn't go into the kitchen and prepare it just five minutes beforehand.

You'd plan, think about it ahead of time, make up a menu. You'd make sure you had the right silverware, that it was polished, dishes and glasses clean and unspotted. You'd go shopping for the food you needed to make the dinner and the dessert. You might think about the music you were going to play, the candles on the table, the flowers you were going to put around the house.

If one would go to this much trouble for a special party, certainly the time invested in a special party with your lover is worth the effort.

We all live in a world where we are too busy. Many couples are simply too active to find time to make love. Both of them work, they have children to take care of, they contribute time and energy to community and church, they are concerned with self-improvement, so they devote several hours a week to health and physical activity, and many have aging parents to look after. The fact is, modern couples are stressed.

The Energy of Love

Making love and going to the gym can provide couples with more energy. But making love requires less effort and is more fun. Better yet, do both. Go to the gym more and have more and better sex.

When partners reduce their lovemaking, they begin the process of starving their love.

Love is nourished by the sexual energy a couple generates.

The withdrawal of sexual energy from a relationship almost certainly spells doom for future happiness.

Without lovemaking, there will be less physical contact, love in an emotional sense will stagnate, and partners will divert their energy elsewhere. If their energy does not go to consuming activities (bowling, golf, bridge, charity work) it goes to other people (lover, mistress, prostitute) whom they naively believe will replace the energy input they are so lacking.

To allow the most important part of life, our significant relationships, to founder and fall apart because we are too busy makes me wonder if our priorities as a society are right. Even though your schedules are busy and it's necessary to work and take care of your family and other responsibilities, it's vitally important to put lovemaking high on any priority list.

If you want to remain together as a couple for a long, long time, then you must nurture and prize the loving aspect of your relationship and give it the energy to sail through the stresses of life that will surely be present from time to time. And this means that on a regular basis you need to prepare for lovemaking at least as thoughtfully as you would for a special occasion. Because it is a special sign of valuing the one you love.

Mental Preparation for Love

You need to start with your mental preparation. You need to turn your mind away from the world's affairs and to each other.

Compare calendars each week to craft your schedule to accommodate your special rendezvous day, time, and place. It doesn't matter which day, but the time must be one in which you can have quiet, privacy, and can allow yourself to turn off all distractions from the outside world. That means phones, beepers, and babies. Turn off the cares and worries of family members who may have health problems, or thoughts of whether you paid your Visa bill on time and whether the company is going to charge interest again. Tune out unwanted stress for this, your appointment with love.

You must free your mind from the mundane distractions of worldly existence and focus lovingly on each other. *And you must make this happen at least once a week.*

If you have children, I certainly understand the problems involved, but you nevertheless need to make arrangements to have them taken care of by a baby-sitter, or to have them visit relatives, or teach them to have respect for Mommy and Daddy's "time-out." That is a moment when you can close and lock the door and children are not only expected but required to leave you alone.

That is perhaps the most difficult thing to accomplish, though I do know couples who regularly set aside the time for Mom and Dad to go into the bedroom and disappear to "take a nap." Others simply go to bed early. If you wait until it gets late and the cat has been put out for the night, you are too sleepy, and being together in any meaningful sense just gets put off. But certainly an hour in the early evening before dinner or not long after it, when both partners can relax and share a moment of loving and tranquility is well worth planning regularly.

Whether it is every day or once a week, during the week or on weekends, you will find you can create an amorous excitement about what's going to happen. Build the heat with seductive messages left on voice mail, e-mail, or in handwritten reminders. Create an anticipation of shared feelings of warmth and love and sexy caring. Part of that expectation means bringing something new and playful into your loving. Build up the tension beforehand. Make a list of erotic surprises for each of you and keep them coming as a regular and special part of your relationship. Send a surprise gift (flowers lingerie, perfumed oil . . .) to her at the office, leave little teasing love notes for him in unexpected places. Excite your lover by being unpredictable and say "I want you inside me" or "I love how I get hot just thinking about tomorrow night."

And remember, neither the man nor woman should think about orgasm, but they should both concentrate on opening each other's minds to being receptive and experiencing their lovemaking as a sensory pursuit, as an adventure, as playful, intimate connection.

THE PURPOSE OF LOVING IS RELATING
PROFOUNDLY TO ANOTHER HUMAN BEING.
ORGASM IS THE BONUS.

Physical Preparation for Love

I strongly suggest that the bedroom be thought of as a kind of temple. Beautify it with lots of candles, works of art, crystal, sensual and seductive draperies, sheets, and bedspreads, and lots of pillows of many sizes, textures, and colors that reflect your own sense of beauty and taste. Don't forget mirrors that can be strategically placed for viewing the action.

Your bedroom should be an aromatic place, the aroma provided sometimes by fresh flowers, sometimes by delicate essential oils in an evaporator, which is available in most health food shops. When heated, these oils fill the room with a sensual odor that helps transport your mind away to some exotic world a million miles from household or business demands.

Incense or Oils

Many people like to use incense. However, incense requires the burning of natural plant substances and fills the room with smoke, which can be irritating to some people. Essential oils placed in an evaporator do a better job with a subtle aroma that permeates every aspect of the senses.

Whether you prefer essential oils or the aromas of incense, the mood of your bedroom needs to be subtle, exciting, and sensual. It should provide an aura of harmony and expectant sexuality. Since the bedroom must always be a place of rest and love, you should never start arguments in the bedroom or take them there. If an argument or disagreement does start, you must immediately leave the bedroom and deal with it outside. Remember, scent goes directly to your central nervous system. Aroma has the power to sooth or stimulate your consciousness.

Lighting

Lighting is important, and candlelight is probably the most desirable and certainly the most romantic light to use. Beautiful candlesticks are an option, but for many the dripping wax of candlesticks and the necessity to remove it on a regular basis is discouraging. Beeswax candles drip less but are more expensive.

Candles in short, thick glasses, both scented and unscented, can be found in most candle shops and supermarkets. They burn for twelve to thirty-six hours, provide a nice warm source of light, are relatively inexpensive, and of course are drip free. They are available in various colors and aromas.

Music

Psychologists tell us that music has profound effects on the subconscious mind. Too often, though, the music we have been taught to think of as loving music, is, in fact, sedating massage music that is more likely to put a tired couple to sleep rather than coincide with their ever-rising and throbbing buildup of sexual tension.

Ideally, your music should be upbeat during foreplay and change in tempo and rhythm with progressive increases in volume and intensity that parallels the developing tension of your sexual encounter, reaching a final crescendo with the thrill of orgasm itself. Change the music again during the romantic lingering of afterplay, similar to that with which you began your loving evening: soft and romantic.

In other words, you should have at least three tapes or CDs. One for the romantic beginning of your loving. A second for the heightened intensity and faster tempo of your sex. And a third for relaxing and savoring the moments after you have both been satisfied.

Music, however, must not be intrusive. You are not at a concert. Your music has to please you but stay in the background.

Music specifically geared for erotic and lovemaking activity has not been a major part of any culture. You need to choose for yourself music you find compatible with your lovemaking style. It could be the music you were listening or dancing to when you first realized you were in love.

The Bedroom of Mrs. Thornton

Chatting one day in my office, Mrs. Thornton told me about the remarkable change in her sex life and her general feeling of being younger and heathier and more in love. She said it was due to the fact that she had redecorated her bedroom.

"Redecorated your bedroom?"

"Yes. It has changed our lives completely."

She described what she had done. "I covered our king-size bed with leopard-print sheets and a wonderful red paisley bedspread with matching and contrasting pillows, at least ten of them in different shapes and sizes, so we are always comfortable no matter what position we get into.

"On either side of the bed I have black lacquer night tables with lamps on a dimmer so I can lower the light from bright to barely on. Just light enough to see each other. It's like a twilight and makes everything look really seductive.

"On one table I've got a CD player with my favorite music. On the other I always put some flowers that I buy that day at the supermarket and, of course, lubricants, oils, and sex toys are waiting for me in a new brass chest I got from a store that sells products from India.

"Above the headboard is a painting of joyous nymphs dancing nude in a woodland setting of reds, greens, and golds. At the foot of the bed is a long, narrow table about the same height as the bed. On it I have a wrought iron candelabrum for five thick candles, several incense burners, and a favorite pair of small statues.

"I hung paintings on the two other walls and put a large mirror strategically on the third. I found a black, flowered, lacquered Oriental screen for one of the corners. Instead of the usual dull venetian blinds, I bought brass-colored ones to cover the two windows.

"It's kind of like a movie set, and my husband has become so sexy and romantic, we're living in a honeymoon state all the time. Just walking through the room stirs me emotionally. It was a lot of trouble, but it was worth every minute and penny I gave to it. Now neither of us can wait to get home from work. What a difference!"

Food

If your romantic interlude is taking place in the evening I think it's a good idea to have a light supper before you make love. It's foolish to have a big dinner. If you eat a big meal before lovemaking, the blood that should concentrate in your pelvic area and genital organs is diverted to your stomach to absorb the food. This reduces the swelling and stimulation of your genitals and makes vigorous movement less comfortable.

However, you may be hungry at the end of the day. So, I suggest you eat a cold shrimp cocktail, clams or oysters on the half shell, some pasta, and perhaps a single glass of wine. Heavy, fatty, creamy meals are definitely out, as they will inhibit the release of the hormones that stimulate lovemaking because the blood circulates to the stomach and stays there longer, detracting from the blood necessary to arouse and engorge your sex organs. All your systems become sluggish, and such meals are not great under any circumstances if you want to stay fit. Speaking of sluggish, while one glass of wine may help relax you after a long day, alcohol is a chemical depressant. You pass out with too much, and excess alcohol before loving dulls your senses as well as your wit.

It's nice sometimes to even have food in the bedroom. You might include fruit like peaches, plums, grapes, cherries, or pomegranates. Or maybe chocolate, honey, or whipped cream, anything that titillates the imagination, whether or not you use them as part of your loving. You might cut an orange in half and squeeze it into each other's mouth—lovingly licking the drips wherever they may fall.

It is also pleasant to have a tiny bottle of concentrated breath freshener containing chlorophyll, which you can place on your tongue to give your mouth a pleasant scent and help make your kisses sweet-smelling and even more irresistible. These drops do wonders for genital kisses too.

The Toy Chest

Finally, of course, preparation should include a well-stocked toy chest. The toy chest is a piece of furniture that you and I are inventing at this moment because everyone needs one and there isn't any specific one on the market. I've seen some very nice brass and wooden chests that can be used for this purpose.

The characteristics of an adult toy chest should be that it is attractive enough to be a piece of furniture in your bedroom and large enough to hold all the accessories for love that one might want to put away in between lovemaking sessions, and lock. These might include, besides your toys, candles, incense sticks, oils, massage oils, creams, and lubricants just about anything you want to keep out of sight and away from the prying eyes of curious children or guests who might be walking through your bedroom. You may want people to assume your toy chest is your blanket chest. Pier 1 and the Bombay Company are good places to begin your search.

And since we are talking about a fun and erotic adventure, you're certainly not going to have enough room in the bedside drawer, or stuffed under the socks and underwear in your dresser, to hold all the delights that are the spices to flavor your loving. So keep your eyes open for a good, pretty, sturdy, lockable chest.

I've also seen inexpensive plastic ones, or simply large storage containers made of PVC that also are able to be locked and perhaps put away in the closet. But whatever kind you choose, you should have a personal and secure place for the accessories of love.

And it should be big enough. Because by the time you are finished with this book, if you truly have incorporated the ideas I think you should be visualizing as we go along, and awakened your imagination to new and ever more creative possibilities, the size and number of items in your toy chest will grow.

The Shopping List

To make all of these preparations, or your own version of them, one partner will need to sit down and do a shopping list, which should include:

- **lubricants**—light and heavy (Astroglide and Vaseline, both available at most drugstores)
- **towels**—ordinary white ones to put on the bed to prevent staining from lubricants and juices, or menstruation. (Yes, it is medically okay to make love while your partner is having her period. Orgasm for her may reduce menstrual cramps as well.)
- **music**—to play in the background
- **candles**—to light the room dimly
- **essential aromatic oils**—to sweeten the air
- **food**—to taste before loving, during loving, or after loving
- **toys**—which I discuss fully in Chapter 15

Your shopping list should also include things necessary for following the bathing ritual. Many can be found in health food shops or department stores.

- **soap**—scented (Dr. Bronner's Peppermint Soap, for example)
- **gel**—(Sensual Bath Gel, available at The Body Shop)
- **oils**—scented or unscented massage oil (Neutrogena Light Sesame Oil [available at the pharmacy], Opium Perfumed Oil Spray, Sensual Oil [available at The Body Shop])
- **creams**—perfumed body cream for variety. Opium Cream or your favorite scent.

creams fortified with vitamins A, E, and aloe vera hand cream for softening your hands which is *very* important. I recommend Neutrogena Hand Cream.

- **powder**—honey dust available through Kama Sutra
- **sponge**—nylon mesh bathing sponge, which you can pour liquid soap or shower gel into and create a wonderfully slippery, bubbly, foamy, sensual, and aromatic lather
- **bath salts**—Borghese and Kama Sutra make great sensual salts
- **bubble bath**—try several and pick your favorite
- **oil of love**—available through Kama Sutra. Apply it to any clean genital or anal area for a unique taste treat. It's available in many flavors, including chocolate mint, orange, vanilla, and cherry.

The Ritual Bath

Your phones are off, your door is locked, your privacy is secure, and your mind is able to focus entirely on the inner dimension of loving. Begin with your bath. It is important, no matter what time of day or night it is, and no matter whether you are dirty or not, that you and your partner bathe together.

The simple purpose: to symbolically wash away the cares of the day.

But first use the toilet so you are sure to have an empty bladder as well as an empty lower rectum in order to be completely comfortable during relaxed and uninhibited sex play. If you are adventurous in your sex play, you might even check by using your finger and, if necessary, take an anal douche to wash away any remnants of stool.

Bodies are not something to be ashamed of. They are to be loved, adored, respected, and cherished.

Now get into the shower together and wash each other slowly

and gently with wonderfully foaming, good-smelling soap. It is tingly and stimulates your skin. It's also slippery and bubbly when used with a net-type body sponge.

The man should start by soaping and massaging the woman's forehead, brows, eyes, nose, cheeks, lips, ears, behind the ears, neck, back of her neck, arms, underarms, shoulders, breasts, stomach, belly button, lower abdomen, buttocks, anus, the crack between her buttocks, clitoris, thighs, lower legs, feet, and toes.

Then she should do the same thing for him. He will certainly take pleasure and amusement in her soaping his penis and butt. This should be done only briefly, or the evening of loving orgasmic sex will explode right there in the shower. For her, the same thing may happen using the shower nozzle or Jacuzzi tub jet.

Now you know your partner's body visually as well as you know your own. You also know it to the touch as well as your own. At the same time that you are soaping, washing, and sliding slippery hands all over each other, ask your partner what feels good and what doesn't so you refine your idea and understanding of his and her erogenous zones.

No book can tell you what feels good to any one person, and more important, erogenous zones change with mood, time, location, age, and experience, so that they are not the same for the same person at different times, and they are not the same for different people.

Always wash the genital area and buttocks carefully. Begin with the outside hair-bearing lips of her vulva with which you should become as familiar as she. Move on to the anal area, which should be washed gently, thoroughly, and pleasurably. A finger may, as I have suggested, be inserted in the anus to check the lower rectum for stool if this is comfortable.

It is important, in my opinion, to make sure the woman's legs are shaved. You know, one of the nicest things a man can do is learn how to shave his lady's legs. She will absolutely adore it if you use some cream and perform this service of love in the shower, being careful not to nick her skin. Take all the time you need.

Then rinse each other carefully.

For showers, I recommend using a shower-head extension with a flexible hose that you can put on the wall and adjust to any height. This allows you to bathe without getting your hair wet if you don't want to and without putting on those frumpy plastic shower caps. Also, being able to direct your jet stream of water is convenient and feels good when rinsing those areas that are most fun.

As you bathe, constantly be aware that you are symbolically washing away, at least for the time being, any troubles you have, thoughts of family or business or whatever detritus dribbles into your brain.

Now it is just the two of you, the two most important people in the world, standing in a womb of love.

Refresh not only your body, but your spirit and soul, a healing cleansing for the loving situation you are creating. Since this is a creative process, this ritualistic bathing is part of that creation and begins to build the excitement and anticipation for the experience you soon will be enjoying.

Having shared the intimacy of your bathing and shaving her, and her bathing you, the rest of the ritual should include the man's shaving his face, since most women do not like the scratches from a day-old beard on their cheeks, breasts, or on the delicate skin between their thighs.

I suggest minimal aftershave, cologne, and deodorant, if any, because these mask natural hormones, odors, and tastes. Needless to say, brushing your teeth and your tongue, using a tongue scraper, will finally make you feel clean, fresh, and alive.

For both lovers I remind you of the importance of trimming and filing your fingernails. Women and men who trim their nails are able to enjoy the sensitivity of their fingertips without the difficulty and limitations that long nails place on truly erotic sex play. Very long nails on women may appear exotic from a distance, but they may feel uncomfortably scratchy or even painful. They are out of place on or in your lover's body.

Shorter nails are sexy. Very long nails are scary.

So, clean, soft hands and short-trimmed nails are a must. Callouses on fingers or feet should be taken care of whenever they appear.

Having completed the bath ritual, it's time to move to the bedroom. If you must cross a living area to do this, wear a robe and don't stop to chat on the way. Entering the scene involves dimming the lights, putting a match to your candles, starting the incense or aromatic oils. The partners may also excuse themselves at this point and dress in a provocative outfit. Something very see-through, lacy, and décolleté for her, silky and inviting for him, teasing the imagination for both. . . .

Or else simply jump into bed comfortable in glorious nakedness.

Part Three

The Doctor's Prescription for Sex Techniques

Chapter 9

Techniques You Need
for Loving

In a new review of American sexual practices reported in the *Journal of the American Medical Association* in February 1999, Dr. Laumann of the University of Chicago and his associates found that forty-three percent of women and thirty-one percent of men suffer from sexual dysfunction. That means between a third and a half of all Americans suffer from the inability to become aroused, the inability to obtain or maintain an erection, the inability to have an orgasm, or the inability to have pleasurable sex due to pain of medical or psychological origin.

"A significant public health concern," is how these researchers describe their startling findings. I call it an alarming epidemic: symptoms of widespread stress, frustration, inhibition, ignorance, and isolation.

No wonder *Time* magazine in an August 2, 1999, article said that "sexual dysfunction has permeated the culture . . . so it's only fitting that TV, long charged with glamorizing lust, is airing images of sex that are not just unglamorous but also neurotic, guilty, antagonistic, even scary."

In addition, a 1999 study released by the MacArthur Foundation found that in looking at eight aspects of quality of life such as sex, children, marriage, and work, *adults gave their sex life the lowest rating of any category.*

These compelling data document unequivocally the call for healing implicit in a recent *New York Times* report that "**what Americans really need is medical help to juice up their sex drives.**" However, the neurotic depiction of sleazy sex on TV, the internet, everywhere, must not be confused with intimate loving lust. People need to "juice-up" their sex drives, **but they need it channeled through the wholesome connection of mind and spirit.**

Advising you to have better loving sex for health, happiness, and longevity without telling you how makes no sense. You need to follow a path; you need a prescription that works. This section shows you how to pull it all together.

There are a myriad of healthy possibilities to jump-start and revitalize your sexuality. You may take some of my suggestions but not all. Those that don't appeal to you now, put away for a rainy day. Have a playful attitude. There is no right or wrong in any sexual activity that doesn't hurt or promote illness.

Remember that sex preferences change over time. They change as your experience grows, or your partner's experience grows, or as your partner changes. It is not necessary to try everything to be a good lover, but you will be surprised how differently you view your body, your partner's body, and the wonderful process of loving if you simply consider the possibilities.

Now, to Begin

One important point is that in any form of lovemaking, male and female partners should switch roles regularly. The man might start as the active giver while the woman is the recipient of tender loving, and then they change roles. When it is the woman's turn, she should take on a more aggressive, genitally focused role.

Most men would like their women to be more aggressive when they are making love. Women should relate to men by moving

toward a more vigorously assertive expression of their sexual desires and willingness to give love. Men should relate to women by moving toward a more sensual and less genitally focused sexuality and a willingness to arouse his partner.

Couples should not persist in trying to stimulate each other at the same time, since it is distracting.

When you are giving loving touches, and your partner's touch, lick, or kiss competes for your attention, it diminishes sensual focus.

Allow yourself a lot of time to feel close and enjoy foreplay. You need to think about the following things you will do, such as kissing.

You might say, "Oh, kissing, I know how to do that. I've been kissing people since I was a child." But erotic kissing is quite another thing.

Kissing

There are five types of kisses:

- **lipping**
  the darker, rougher part of your lip and the soft, moist pinker part of your lip are placed against those of your partner's upper and lower lips in repeated gestures as though eating a pudding that is falling off a spoon.
- **tonguing**
  insert your tongue in your partner's mouth. This is also called French kissing. Remember we discussed earlier that the saliva from the glands under your tongue is extremely sweet, so if you are going to tongue someone, you might think of sucking some saliva up and swallowing it until you get to the sweet, delicious saliva from these glands. Tonguing then becomes more delightful because taste is added to the

sensation of tongue touch. The line underneath the tongue that goes from the tip to the back is particularly sensitive, as is the similar line above the front teeth under the upper lip.

- **love biting and nibbling**
  love bites may be soft or hard but in no case should break the skin or leave a mark. In a recent James Bond film, *Tomorrow Never Dies,* Pierce Brosnan actually bites his costar's lip, she admitted during a TV interview, and said she loved the animal quality of it. It should be remembered some skin is more sensitive to bruising than others, and care must be taken to give your love bites in ways acknowledged as pleasurable by your partner. Bioflavenoids and natural vitamin C reduce easy bruising.

- **sucking**
  a sucking kiss is the opposite of a tonguing kiss. It can be used to suck your partner's tongue, toes, an earlobe, nipple, the clitoris, the penis, or almost any place. Sucking kisses can vary in intensity. However, sucking hard for a long time may result in a bruise, which usually fades in several days to a week.

- **blowing**
  this kiss involves gently blowing. An example of this would be grasping the aroused erect nipple of her breast between your teeth lightly, lipping it with a lipping kiss, then blowing while exhaling over the moistened nipple or inhaling and sucking in the air over the moistened nipple, both of which can be especially arousing.

Once again, be sure to change what you are doing, and switch frequently who plays the active role, and who is on the receiving end as you make love.

Touching

Touching is probably the single most important part of loving.
It starts with the warm, reassuring embrace that should be shared
every day between loving partners upon awakening. This embrace
is called the Spiritual Spoon. Try it tomorrow morning as soon as
the alarm goes off before you get up. It takes only a few minutes but
is a most exquisite, loving way to start the day, and it will give you
the emotional strength to help meet any problems that arise.

- **The Spiritual Spoon**
    The couple lie in a nurturing, spoonlike position on
    their sides. The emotionally stronger partner at that
    particular moment takes the back place of the spoon
    and the emotionally more fragile should take the inner
    place. In other words, the stronger partner curls his or
    her chest and belly along the other partner's back, and
    they lock together.

    The person in back wraps his or her hands around
    the inner person, placing a hand over their heart. They
    remain in this mode for five minutes. The warmth of
    skin against skin establishes a mind/body/spirit con-
    nection that allows both partners to feel emotionally
    secure, their relationship steeped in personal confi-
    dence and trust. This kind of energy exchange should
    become a regular morning habit.

    On a recent Barbara Walters interview show, Bar-
    bra Streisand bragged to viewers that she and the im-
    portant man in her life, James Brolin, whom she later
    married, always "spooned."

    "Spooned?"

    "You know, spooned," she repeated.

Now you know what she meant, if you didn't already, and you can do what the stars do.

- **The healing touch**

    Touching all over the body is healing.

    Many modern alternative medicine advocates use the healing nature of the touch of their hands in order to treat patients for a variety of ailments.

    Reiki, for example, is one of the oldest schools of healing touch, dating back two thousand years. It demonstrates, without a doubt, the importance of touch in creating states of well-being. I have seen many examples of the laying on of hands actually giving life to people. Any of several touching techniques work by awakening and directing energy from or through our bodies to heal.

- **The energy of touching—active touching, active receiving.**

    The body contains the energy of our life force. As long as we live, we emanate that energy. It manifests itself as a field or aura surrounding us. The flow of this energy can be consciously aroused and directed. For example, you may visualize an energy flow coming from your hands and fingers when you touch your lover.

    It is extremely important to realize that this connection cannot be a one-way street. That is, the recipient must actively desire to feel and respond to the sensual touch and the energies given by his or her partner, and the giver must actively and consciously intend to give this energy to nourish, love, and arouse his partner.

    Thus, touching is never static, even when your hands are still, because you are passing and exchanging energy in a loving way.

- **The erotic touch**

    There are many books and videotapes out about

erotic massage and much conversation goes on about it. But it is quite different from a normal massage. A regular massage such as one you might get from a certified massage therapist is an excellent form of relaxing. It is generally done to very quieting New Age music that is sleepy rather than stimulating. Its purpose is the same as what you do after a bath when you massage cream into your skin. It squeezes the toxic accumulations of metabolism from the spaces between your cells, under your skin, and in your muscles and sends the poisons into the lymphatic system, where they are carried to the excretory organs of the skin, liver, and kidneys.

This is a wonderful thing. However, it is not stimulating and arousing as a method of foreplay for sex. Needless to say, just as you don't want sedating music, you don't want to give your partner a tranquilizing massage before you make love, because that would numb the senses and dull responsivity to the lightest of touches and the most sensitive of moments.

Quite the contrary, you want all senses alert, alive, and able to focus. So a massage in the context of the loving touch is quite a different thing. And it involves touching in an erotic fashion with the intention to arouse your partner's erogenous zones.

This is a give-and-take communication since your partner needs to tell or show you the map of where his or her erogenous zones are. And you need to listen to the messages you are given. Show your partner what you like and what you don't like in a gentle, positive way so as not to hurt any feelings. Show by describing. Show by example. Show by directing his or her hands or by noises you make that reveal your satisfaction.

- **The stationary touch**

   Touch may be stationary. A stationary touch is simply putting your hand on a person and leaving it there as you did in the spoon position. You might place your hand on their forehead, on their chest over their heart, on their abdomen, buttocks, back, wherever.

   Stationary touches with the intention of energy transmission can be very, very healing and very positive. However, the flow of healing positive energy through a stationary touch is something that must be practiced and nurtured with both partners' concentrating on feeling their energy mingling and shooting from one to the other.

- **The moving touch**

   Then there is the moving touch. You may move your hand lightly or firmly, in a circle, a line, or a pattern, generally using your fingertips and the palm or heel of the hand, or sometimes a whole arm.

- **The squeezing touch**

   There is the squeezing, kneading, or gentle pushing touch.

- **The scratching touch**

   And the scratching touch, which, like the biting kiss, should not, in a frenzy of emotion, be taken to the extreme of drawing blood.

- **The tapping touch**

   The tapping, slapping, or pinching touch are all variations to be tried and enjoyed.

So, however you touch, touch with thought, love, and with the conscious intention of stimulating, arousing, and communicating love to your partner. Let yourself express your emotions with touching and kissing, licking and biting, probing with your tongue and sucking. At the same time, use your fingers to playfully increase excitement.

The Art of Touching

When a man bestows a long, smooth caress with the palm of his hand over his beloved's breast, back, and down her buttocks and continues down her thighs with the lightest possible brushing of his fingertips, he is conscious of purposefully igniting her, arousing her passion with sexual energy from his touch.

As you give pleasure to your partner with your touch, you also receive sexual pleasure from the contact and sensory feedback from your fingertips as they brush across his or her body.

You, the giver, sensing your lover's skin against your hand, delight in the feel of its texture, its softness, its firmness, its moistness, its warmth, and the energy it emits. You delight, too, in the reaction you get as your lover grows more and more aroused in movements, bodily changes that reflect arousal—color change and swelling of the labia, a flush of the chest skin, an increase in breathing rate, and the sounds of love that tell you that things are going well.

But no matter how good the technique or how loving the caress, if he or she is not consciously receptive, if the mind is a zillion miles away, nothing will happen. One partner must be as conscious of the gift offered as the other one is of bestowing it. **Ultimately it is the mind that directs the touch, and it is the mind that accepts it.**

The Masturbating Touch

While masturbation is usually considered a solo activity, many will find delight in the pleasure their partner takes when they masturbate themselves during sex play. Men and women alike enjoy watching their lovers play with themselves as a type of foreplay.

A woman can touch herself in a way that pleases her while her man is making love to her with his penis, fingers, or toys inside her.

This is a practical as well as erotic technique, since most women know how to give themselves great pleasure with their own touch.

Stimulating her own clitoris, for example, frequently results in vaginal contractions that are of great delight to her partner. Her own touch combined with his penis inside can be sublime.

If his woman sometimes masturbates to orgasm as entertaining foreplay, perhaps with her man playing an assisting role with his finger or tongue, it frequently takes the pressure off his performing, of feeling responsible for giving his lover an orgasm. It will allow him to enjoy his erotic pleasure more, knowing his partner is satisfied, relaxed, and happy . . . and, perhaps, that twinkle in her eye and sultry smile may mean she's ready for more!

Chapter 10

The Art
of Sexual Intercourse
and How to Find
the G-spot

Anyone who has ever made love to a partner or had someone make love to them will recognize that lovemaking is an art, and the better it is done, the more arousing the variations, the more passionate and satisfying it will be. It is an art that is learned, not inherited.

Points to Remember

Several points should be emphasized with regard to intercourse:

1. NEVER take a goal-oriented approach where the sole purpose of loving is to reach orgasm. Actually, knowing that you don't have to have an orgasm to enjoy your erotic interludes will, in the end, lift the tension some feel when they think they have to perform. You won't need to fake it, as some women and men do or else be judged a failure, and ironically, it will make it that much easier to have your orgasm.

You might have a fantastic evening of love where you or your partner *don't* have an orgasm.

2. It is always important to vary postures, positions, movements, speeds, and touches in such a way as to prolong the experience of intimacy and prolong the development of sexual tension. This will add to the quality and strength of your orgasms.

3. Remember what you did when you set the scene for love? Remember to use all your senses of taste, touch, sight, sound, and smell as you reach out to your lover. A hot touch may be more exciting than a cool kiss. A single flower or favorite music will go a long way toward creating the mood.

4. Communication during lovemaking is important. These are verbal affirmations of love. For example, at a particularly exciting moment you might gasp, "Darling, oh, darling" or "Sweetheart," and say your lover's name, or simply sigh and moan as you exhale in your love language. Some enjoy "dirty talk," which is fine.

And there are nonverbal affirmations of love, such as the way you touch, the intensity with which you kiss, and the way you look at each other. A look with deepening warmth and affection can be as emotional as a touch.

Closing your eyes during lovemaking is quite common, probably because it is easier to have a fantasy, which, as I have said, is great. However, it shuts out your lover and creates darkness. Lovers should try to maintain contact with each other in as many ways as possible during their lovemaking. People often remark, "I could see the love in her eyes, the way she looked at him."

Eyes are the window to the soul.

The eyes of your lover are the windows to the ecstasy you share, and you should keep yours open and look deeply into your lover's eyes as often as possible.

Basic Positions

The standard positions are quite familiar. The variations of different positions are endless. They are described in the *Kama Sutra* and in a great number of more recent books published in England and the United States. You can get them all in your bookstore. Many of the books show exactly the same thing. So it becomes a matter of choosing which artist or photographer or models you prefer.

But some books and magazines go out of their way to look for something new and end by describing positions that are dangerous to your balance and back or downright funny and uncomfortable.

Because information on postions is readily available, I will not go into detail on this subject but will give you the basics:

1. Horizontal with the male on top
2. Horizontal with the female on the top
3. Side by side with partners facing
4. Side by side with one partner behind—lying, kneeling, standing, sitting
5. The female partner sits on the male with her legs crossed around him, her arms embracing him, and the male sits with his legs crossed supporting her buttocks. Her body, chest, breasts, head, and face are all in contact with him. This is a very intimate form of loving.
6. Male sitting in a chair with partner on top facing toward or away from him.

Moving

Let's shift from positions to how to move. According to ancient literature, there are one thousand and one movements. But that is only an amusing estimate of what is really an infinite number of ways of moving.

The basic ways of moving include:

1. Pelvic thrusting
2. Pelvic circling
3. Side to side
4. Male moving back and forth in the female's vagina. The female moving back and forth on the male's penis.

The most stimulating movements for the woman are those that involve shallow penetration and movements in the lower third of the vagina, where the Love Muscles are in contact with the penis. This is because the deeper parts of the vagina open during arousal and stimulation to form basically an empty space or container and do not grasp or surround the penis with contact. The air that goes in it may come out as a "vart," or vaginal fart, when the woman changes position.

The Woman on Top

Before leaving the subject of positions and moving, I would like to discuss briefly position number two with the female on top. Some women may feel initially awkward, embarrassed, or self-conscious about assuming the lead in performing various pelvic movements, especially if they are on top, because they have long become entangled in the propaganda that the woman's role should be submissive.

Women should persevere and emerge from that old way of thinking and acting and their men should encourage such a break from the past. This awkwardness will quickly dissolve as embarrassment becomes a flush of arousal for women who allow themselves to take their own pleasure by being on top and in a *controlling* posture for sexual intercourse. Not only does she have the opportunity to lead, she also can teach her partner the movements she likes and she can control the depth of penetration into her vagina.

For a lot of men, taking the lead is a measure of their masculinity, their ego, how macho they are, and they may even feel threatened by a woman who takes this kind of major role in lovemaking.

These men must realize how limiting it is always to be the director and giver. It means he never knows what a joy it is to lie back and be made love to. It means he will never see her find her own satisfaction, moving in a way that excites her, which can be a wonderful source of instruction for the man as well as a highly erotic experience for both partners.

When a woman makes love to a man, she not only delights him, she shows him what most gives her pleasure. How soon she wants to leave their foreplay and take the next step, the kind of connection she seeks with him, the angle of entry she uses to take his penis into her. These are all nonverbal instructions, just as kissing or touching are steps in the dance of love.

So she expresses her loving with her own movements and behavior: a shallow, teasing rubbing of her vaginal lips against his body, then allowing a short, shallow penetration of his penis into the first inch of her vagina, which is the most sensitive, and an intermittent deep penetration. Especially if a woman has ridden horses as a child or adolescent, her movements may be very facile and sophisticated. This is because the pelvic rocking motion that is so exciting to the penis also rubs the back of the penile shaft and testicles between the cheeks of her buttocks.

The Circle Dance

As the woman makes love to her man, who lies beneath her, she may enjoy manually massaging her clitoris. It is also important for her to try other movements instead of the old-fashioned in and out. These include circular movements, clockwise and counterclockwise,

or side-to-side movements, all of which bring pleasure to both partners.

This is how a woman might use the circular movement as she
makes love to her man. He lies on his back with a pillow under his
buttocks to raise his genitals, while the woman sits on top of him
with his penis inside her.

She moves her pelvis and hips in a full circular motion at various
speeds, both lifting and lowering herself as she moves, and varying
the angle of her dance by leaning toward or away from him. She
may also turn around while still sitting and face away from him
toward his feet.

These techniques give a wonderful physical sensation to the man,
and also to the woman, who will enjoy this opportunity to be in
control. As she performs this dance over her lover, she should be
especially conscious of what feels good to her and let her lover
know by eye contact and by the sounds and words of love that she
offers.

In this position the man may actively help his lover make the
movements that feel best. He may move his hips, but more likely **he
will use his hands to hold her hips and move her** in a motion that
feels particularly good. This is generally well liked by both partners.

With the woman on top, the penis moves in and out of the vagina
at a very acute angle. Thus the head of the penis puts substantial
pressure on the woman's G-spot, and as it is moving out, moves
over her perineal area between her buttocks, which also gives a
unique sensation to both his testicles and the shaft of his penis.

While extraordinary sexual entanglements and positions can be
seen in all sorts of old manuscripts and on walls of ancient villas
like those of the first-century Italian city of Pompeii, it is better to
think of them as symbols of ecstatic ritual than to attempt to copy
them. The postures and positions you discover with your partner
should be those that are comfortable and variations of the five basic
postures described above. Comfort for lovers is critical and plenty
of pillows should be available. Care should be taken not to lean too
heavily on the woman in some of the positions.

It is a good idea to shift positions now and then, preferably without the penis being withdrawn from the vagina, in order to avoid muscle cramping and to allow prolonged lovemaking. If both partners move together and the woman pushes or presses herself closer to the man in order to maintain a tight contact as they roll over and the other one moves to the top, they won't have to break their magic love connection.

Speed

Speed is a vital characteristic of movement. During intercourse, you should consciously vary the speed from slow to fast and back again. **Nonmovement** is also a type of movement. When the man uses his Love Muscles to contract and pulsate and bob his penis inside her and she uses her Love Muscles to contract on his penis, the couple can become expert in Love Muscle manipulation and internal movement to their delight without a lot of external movement. This is especially easy with trained and exercised Love Muscles. (See Chapter 14 for exercises.)

The Clitoris

As you know by now, this most sensitive organ sits on top of the vulva like a jewel.

The clitoris is the only organ in the body whose sole purpose is to generate pleasure.

Although in most women the tip of the clitoris is tiny, its shaft extends an inch or so up like the shaft of the penis. It is, in fact, the embryological equivalent of the penis, as you have seen in the illustrations. Learning the right clitoral touch is important. Overstimulation of the clitoris can short-circuit the woman's energy. The right touch is something a woman must learn by herself and should then pass on to her lover by showing him how to stroke, press, rub, tap, or lick her clitoris in the best way.

How to Find the G-spot

The G-spot was named after the German-born gynecologist Ernst Gräfenberg, who died in 1957. He is credited with having been the first to describe it as erectile and highly erogenous tissue. The G-spot is not a magic, excitable point in every woman's body. It is an energetic spot located in different places in different women. In fact, some women claim they are finding other spots that they are giving different letters and names to.

In any case, while the clitoris is outside and exposed, the G-spot is deep inside and protected. Once located, it is a place that can produce profound pleasure. Finding the G-spot is often difficult for a woman to accomplish alone, though in examining her body, she may have found it. In some positions she can just about reach it, but it will be awkward because it is at the top of the front of her vagina, somewhere between the middle third and the base of the cervix. A few women have told me they could find the spot by squatting and pressing toward the navel with two fingers inside them and then making a come-hither motion with these fingers.

For most women, identifying and awakening the G-spot requires the loving touch of her partner. She can lie on her back with her legs raised so that one or both of her legs rests against her lover's chest or shoulders, He might kneel beside her on the floor, or he can sit cross-legged between her legs with her buttocks up on a pillow.

- Her vagina should be well lubricated, and the first few times you try this, it should be completely as an experiment.
- The man should use two fingers.
- Slip the fingers gently in and curl them so the pads of the fingers stroke the front wall of the vagina in a

come-hither motion, moving from the cervix to the entry near the urethral opening. (See Fig. 3.)

- Caress the wall with long smooth strokes and follow the entire vagina from the cervix to the urethra. Most women will be able to identify a spot that is intensely stimulating about halfway down.
- With the heel of the other hand, the man should put a gentle pressure on the clitoris at the same time. Do this for ten to thirty seconds.

Some women may feel a little pain or that they have to urinate. Such spasms quickly pass when there is enough time for the woman to become comfortable with the new sensations. This may not happen right away and it may take weeks or even months before great pleasure can be enjoyed from this area. The man should lighten his touch if discomfort is felt or withdraw if he needs to reassure his partner.

The G-spot can usually take longer periods of stimulation than the clitoris can without getting over-stimulated, but in the beginning the man must be ho]extremely gentle. His purpose should not be to push her to orgasm but, rather, to bring her a pleasurable sensation and to connect with her and develop a map of her sensitive vaginal areas.

- Once the man has found the G-spot, he should stop. The two fingers of his right hand should remain inside her vagina, gently on the spot, while the other hand exerts pressure with the thumb or two fingers on the clitoris.
- Lovers should maintain eye contact and breathe together while doing this.
- After a moment or two, the man may again gently stroke the spot for several minutes and then stop again and be still.
- He can again apply stimulation to the clitoris at this

point, but he should remember that he is stimulating two very powerful poles simultaneously and it may be almost too much and may result in overstimulation.

- It is usually better to alternate stimulating the clitoris and the G-spot and maintain a balance of stillness and movement.

- This should be performed in cycles and repeated for several rounds. The number can be increased over time.

- The combination of focusing your mind on your partner's pleasure, and balancing stillness with movement, increases the intensity of loving immeasurably.

- The G-spot may also be felt anally with lots of lubrication. Some women find this the most pleasurable way. The man must use separate fingers for this type of lovemaking, as it is important *not* to introduce bacteria from the anus into the vagina.

- He should insert his finger or fingers into his lover's anus and, using the same come-hither motion, find the G-spot by pressing the front wall of the anus forward to the pubic bone. In either case, he must take time and be gentle.

This is what sexual growth is all about, learning to do it right and do it better.

The Afterglow

It is important to realize that there is still great potential in the afterglow of lovemaking . . . when the dance is over. This is a time when the man is most empty of energy but also most receptive.

A woman, on the other hand, is quite energized at this moment. In order to emphasize their love, the man may remain inside his beloved even though he has ejaculated and is now soft. It is a time of tremendous intimacy.

When a couple wants to share this intimacy, it is important to stay locked together, because it keeps passion perking under the surface. The moments after orgasm connect a couple in a sexual union, bathed in an afterglow of luminescent harmony and spiritual closeness. It solidifies your relationship and honors your feeling for each other. Keep the caressing and kissing going after orgasm.

During all loving, words and sounds go straight to the heart, and to the **subconscious** mind. Thus the physical, psychic, and spiritual exchanges preceding orgasm build tension and energy. With orgasm there is a release of that energy with a sudden explosive force that literally rips through one's consciousness and explodes the mind and spirit into stars.

Sexual sharing to the point of orgasm is the greatest of blessings. The act of love is truly the devotion to existence and an affirmation of life.

Chapter 11

Oral Sex
for Women

Experimenting with oral lovemaking can be incredibly exciting. Sexual sharing of every possible type can only make the life we have on earth, and the love we feel for another person, that much sweeter.

Loving is a life and health-promoting activity, one sign of which is an open, positive, and creative attitude. Sex in which neither partner is hurt, diminished, or degraded can only be good.

Oral sex is medically safe, physically delightful, and practical.

Yet for some modern couples, learning oral techniques means going against the prejudices that may have been ingrained since childhood. It is important to cast away these outmoded ideas and consider oral sex in its wonderful, pleasure-giving, and healing capacity.

Because of hangups about licking, nibbling, and tasting these areas, or swallowing ejaculate from the penis, fewer people engage in oral sex than in intercourse. According to *Sex in America,* seventy-seven percent of men and only sixty-eight percent of women have tried oral sex in their lifetimes.

It is time to overcome shyness about oral sex.

Because a woman's sexual organs are hidden and more private, it may seem embarrassing to her if a lover kisses and massages her vulva and vagina when she rarely, if ever, has seen them herself. Thus I heartily recommend that women make that special effort to explore their bodies that I recommended in Chapter 6.

His-and-Her Oral Sex

Testosterone is the primary sex hormone of men and the primary hormone of aggressiveness as well. Thus, men may frequently be too assertive, harsh, and hard in their loving. Women tend to be too timid, receptive, diffuse, and more soft, fuzzy, cuddly, and shy in their focus. They have a total body orientation as opposed to a genital one.

Because of this, most men say women give oral sex with too much passivity and too little activity. Too much slow movement and not enough, firm, fast, hard movement. Too little sucking rather than too much. Basically, too little rather than too much of everything.

With regard to oral sex, most women say that their men get carried away, are too orgasmically focused, spend too much time in one spot, tend to be a little too rough in all areas.

It is important, therefore, that both sexes attempt to understand the nature of their bodies, to communicate with sight, sound, and gentle hand direction or masturbating in front of their lover, their wishes concerning touching, kissing, stroking, sucking, and licking in oral sex.

Cunnilingus

This is a funny name for a delightful way of making love. The word does have a logic to it. In Latin it means "vulva licker," which is exactly what it is. The man licks, sucks, and gently nibbles his

lover's vulva and clitoris, as well as her inner thigh, the crack between her buttocks, and the area from her vagina to her anus.

The first point to remember is that the giver of oral sex must
always **find a comfortable position.** This may easily be accomplished in bed by lifting her hips up with several pillows or by
holding her buttocks with your two hands while supporting your
elbows on the bed. This puts the weight of her trunk directly on
your arms and requires no muscle straining. She is, of course, lying
on her back and you are lying on your stomach, your face between
her legs, where you can easily reach the labia and clitoral area, the
area between the vagina and anus, and the anus itself.

Although your hands are not free because they are holding her
buttocks, you can position her vulva, her outer genital area, where
you want it against your mouth and suck and lick it.

The position where your partner is raised up on pillows also
enables you to touch her vagina and abdomen, breasts and other
erotic areas. This is much more comfortable than when the woman
is lying flat on her back and her partner is flat on his stomach with
his head bent backward at her vulva.

Other positions that are comfortable and allow you to enjoy a
leisurely interlude of cunnilingus are placing the woman on her
back on the edge of the bed with her legs up while you sit on a
pillow on the floor next to the bed with your head facing her bottom.

Another variation that allows you to have access to your lover
with your tongue and mouth and at the same time have your hands
free to play with her is for the woman to sit in a chair while you sit
on a pillow on the floor. This can be quite comfortable if you pick a
chair with the right height.

Alternatively, you might try having the woman kneel over your
face while you lie on your back, your head underneath her, between
her legs. In this position her vulva, vagina, and clitoris are directly
over your mouth. This posture allows her to lower herself on your
mouth and apply varying pressures, speeds, and movement while
facing top or feet.

The positions I have just described of loving your woman's vulva and bottom are better than just lying uninspiredly in bed. They are more fun, and will provide the comfort that allow both partners to focus on the pleasure they are experiencing.

Techniques and Advice for Men

The Tongue

Kiss, suck, lick, and blow on her clitoris the way you would like to have your penis kissed, sucked, and licked. The head of the clitoris is just as sensitive as the head of the penis, and the shaft of the clitoris responds to stroking, sucking, and licking just as the penis does.

Remember, just as you find it delightful to have the area around your penis and behind it kissed and licked, your woman enjoys the same attention to the area around her clitoris. Continuous stimulation of one area, though, may stop the step-by-step elevation of arousal that leads to fantastic sex. Therefore, it's important not to remain in one place for more than a minute or two but to change location, rate, speed, and pressure. Variety is, after all, the spice of mental and sexual stimulation.

You must take seriously the communication you receive from your partner during oral sex. Those moans, groans, sighs, sounds, and words of love, those pelvic and hand movements she makes that gently guide you toward the spot where she feels the most excitement and which is most arousing. Moans are love language for you to learn from and respond to.

Techniques for Men to Follow

- Lick her clitoris
- Suck the shaft of her clitoris
- Suck and drag your teeth very gently across the shaft of the clitoris

- Suck while flicking the tip of your tongue horizontally or vertically across the end of her stimulated clitoris, making the clitoris swell just like the penis does during arousal. This is called butterfly kissing and excites a woman as much as it would a man.
- Suck her outer lips and the inner lips, lick them, kiss them, taste them. Don't forget the vaginal opening itself and the spot between the vagina and the rectum as well. It's a natural, healthy experience.
- Try anointing her with chocolate, "honey dust," or whipped cream. Savor the sweet taste of it.

  At the same time that you are licking and sucking her clitoris, you may insert two fingers (one is generally not quite enough) into her vagina and stimulate her inside, including her G-spot. When you arrive at this exquisitely sensitive area, the woman should let you know by a moan or groan or words as she exhales to show that you have touched an area that gives her great pleasure.

With practice you can arouse and stop, change position and movement, so you bring her level of excitement to ever-increasing heights of stimulation called plateaus and build upon the existing tension, layer upon layer, until she is able to experience explosive orgasms. There is hardly any limitation to what can be tried if you have the imagination and desire and enjoy the playfulness of experimentation.

After you have performed oral sex for a while, change positions and have vaginal intercourse. Then change positions again and have oral sex again, always with the intention of avoiding immediate orgasm so that you bring each other to an almost unbearable peak of excitement and anticipation. Feeling her partner's warm tongue licking and sucking and moving over her clitoris may be one of the most exciting and personal demonstrations of love that a woman can receive from her partner.

Female Ejaculation—Does It Exist?

Just as men have a dewdrop of crystal-clear, sweet secretion with intense arousal but before ejaculation, so women may secrete a clear sweet fluid before orgasm. There is a natural vaginal taste that may vary from neutral to slightly sweet with a sour tinge. This is because the normal bacteria in the vagina ferment the starch in the vaginal epithelial cells into lactic acid, creating a slight acidity of the vagina.

The lubrication in the woman's vagina is probably due to the seeping of clear fluid from the vaginal walls and the secretion from glands surrounding the entrance to the vagina, including the glands around the opening of the urethra (such as the Bartholin's, and Skene's glands). This is a result of the intense blood flow of the pelvis and vaginal skin. This is *not* equivalent to a male ejaculation because there is no seminal vesicle (a woman's eggs are in her ovaries and don't travel in secreted fluid), no prostate gland, and no muscles that contract and expel fluid from the vagina or any of the *glands* around the vagina. **This simply does not exist.** There are, however, muscles around the base of the bladder, the bladder itself, the entrance of the vagina for the first two inches, and the rectum that do undergo intense spasms during orgasm.

The fluid that is secreted or even squirted by some women during some orgasms is a mixture of some vaginal and glandular secretion but mostly urine suddenly expelled through the urethral opening from the bladder due to spasms of the bladder muscle that are part of Love Muscle spasms.

Both men and women can have orgasms without the ejaculation of fluid. They are separate functions, though obviously when there is ejaculation, orgasm causes it. Some people do not accept the fact that ejaculation in women is part urine, which is sterile and can be tasted or even drunk without any medical harm. Since it is not a very sexy explanation, many women feel they would rather imagine some more exotic glandular source.

The human anatomy, however, does not justify this conclusion.

While the man may not wish to drink her "ejaculation," it certainly is a reflection of intense orgasm on the part of the female. Some women produce as little as a fraction of a teaspoon, while others as much as half a cup. It may not occur all the time in women who have it, and it is not produced by all women.

Placing extra white towels under her may reassure the woman who has copious "ejaculations," which she suppresses for fear of producing puddles of fluid on the sheets. The man's acceptance of such preparation shows a loving attitude that tells her that she is desired and that he understands.

Know your body and the look and taste of ecstasy.

Chapter 12

Oral Sex
for Men

Fellatio, another strange word we use, means in Latin "to suck." The technique of fellatio, or oral stimulation to the penis, consists of licking and sucking the penis. Sucking is one of our most primitive instincts, so it can become quite natural once you try it.

While sucking the penis, the woman may roll her tongue around the head of the penis or probe gently with her tongue into the small urethral opening at the tip. You should also try increasing and decreasing suction, increasing it as you withdraw the penis from your mouth. Sometimes men like a light dragging of your teeth against the skin of the penis for variety. Then move your tongue back and forth down the length of the penis. It can be held in one or both hands to steady it or to simultaneously stroke it while sucking and also to keep it at the proper angle to be comfortable.

Remember, the penis should be caressed and sucked in the position in which it is normally erect.

A woman should look at a man's erection and hold the penis in a similar position when performing oral sex on it. Even though it can be bent straight out or downward, these are abnormal positions and obstruct the flow of blood, just as kinking a garden hose obstructs the flow of water.

In an abnormally bent or kinked position, the erection is decreased and it is more difficult to ejaculate. Most women fail to understand this simple fact and most men are unaware of it or too distracted to point it out.

It's important to vary what you do.

Techniques

1. Use the tip of your tongue to gently probe, tickle, and circle the head of the penis.
2. Suck the head and the shaft with different degrees of force.
3. Alternately kiss the sides and shaft of the penis.
4. Carefully press the penis so you can feel the two large, swollen, cylindrical tubes on either side, which are filled with blood and cause the erection. There is a small dent or valley the length of the penis on the underside between them. Feel this area with your fingers. This area is particularly sensitive because there is a confluence of nerves as well as blood vessels that travel up and down the underside of the penis. It is important to understand this, so when sucking the penis you can rub your tongue up and down along the back undersurface and superstimulate this very erotic area.
5. As the man can when giving oral sex to a woman, the woman can try putting a few drops of chlorophyll-containing breath freshener or mouthwash on her tongue and then take his penis into her mouth.

The Hidden Penis

Remember, too, the last third of the penis, the hidden part behind the testicles that extends toward the anus. To feel this, put your fingers gently between the testicles and push up toward the anus. Ask the man to squeeze his Love Muscles by making the clenching motion as if to stop urination. You'll easily feel this hidden penis move.

The Tip of the Penis

The tip of the penis is the most sensitive part, just like the tip of the clitoris. There is no need to swallow the entire penis and, as a matter of fact, it is usually impossible, though you can train yourself to suppress the gag reflex. But the most sensitive parts are in its end anyway. And because of the natural angle, the penis usually goes up to the roof of the woman's mouth rather than down toward the back of her throat, except in the 69 position with the woman's bottom facing her partner's head.

Stroking the Penis

While sucking, licking, and occasionally gently stroking with her teeth, the woman may also stimulate the penis by kneading her hand or hands on its base, around the testicles and in the area between the testicles and the anus known in acupuncture as the Hun Yin, or love spot. It is also pleasant for your lover when you suck and caress one or both testicles and take one or both in your mouth and tickle them gently, though remember this is a particularly sensitive area and easily prone to discomfort rather than stimulation.

Tasting the Ejaculate

One of the things many women are concerned about is what to do when a man comes inside her mouth. The fluid that shoots out when he ejaculates may vary in quantity from one to five cc's, or enough to fill a tablespoon. It varies in taste from bland to sweet to slightly bitter. It may also vary in consistency from thick to very liquid, though it usually changes consistency and thickens to a gel after it is ejaculated.

It has been reported that altering a man's diet can affect the taste of his semen. Therefore, if you find your lover's semen has a taste that isn't pleasant, changing his diet may change the taste so it becomes more palatable. Truly unpleasant-tasting semen or foul-smelling semen is rare, is usually a sign of infection, and the man should see a urologist.

To Swallow or Not to Swallow

Semen contains protein, amino acids, trace elements, and minerals. It is sterile and is healthy to swallow. However, many women find difficulty with the idea of swallowing the ejaculate or having the penis in her mouth when a man comes. With practice and familiarity, you can please your lover, receiving his ejaculation with love rather than rejection, and can swallow it without worry.

While some women may be afraid to swallow because of distress or worry about dirtiness, finding the whole idea disgusting, it really is such a normal extension of this type of loving that to become inhibited at the point where your lover is reaching the ecstatic feelings you have helped him to attain seems unfortunate.

It may well take a conscious effort to overcome longstanding inhibitions in order to bring yourself to the point where you can freely and joyously accept swallowing your partner's ejaculate. This may require time and patience for both people, but it should nevertheless be a goal and something a woman can do to increase the variety and excitement in her love life.

For some the taste is pleasant. For others, it becomes an acquired taste like champagne. I remember the first time I was given a sip of champagne as a child, I thought it was awful and couldn't figure out what the adults were all raving about. In time, and with some practice, I did acquire the taste and now toast with champagne with as much gusto as anyone, though I confess it is not my first choice, as your lover's ejaculate may not be yours. Then again, it may become your favorite.

In any case, give it a chance.

If this is your first time trying oral sex, don't ask your lover to withdraw before he comes, and don't spit out his ejaculate after he comes in your mouth. Try drinking in your love for him. Of course, whether or not you want your lover to ejaculate in your mouth is something the two of you should think about and discuss *in advance*.

It is a good idea to try to familiarize yourself with a man's ejaculation before deciding whether you can swallow it. If you are hesitant about swallowing because of the taste or fear you might cough or gag and offend your lover, start out tasting just a little portion until you become accustomed to it. Then you will know what to expect when giving oral sex.

If you simply can't get over your inhibitions or hesitancy, discuss this with him so that he can share with you the decision about what to do. You might spit out his come on a discreetly placed towel kept under a pillow, have him withdraw from your mouth before ejaculation and finish him off with your hand, or whatever you both agree will work.

Ideally, the woman should feel "I accept this sweetness from you" as you taste and swallow his fluid of love.

It is the goal of loving to be able to accept freely all forms of orgasm and ejaculation.

Advantages of Fellatio

If a woman enjoys having her man's tongue lick and caress her, she should be willing to, and hopefully enjoy, licking and caressing him too. So, I encourage women to approach fellatio with a free, open, and playful attitude, to overcome any personal hurts such as being forced to perform this act in the past, and to fully enjoy yourself with someone you care about deeply. It is a loving and dramatic way for a woman to show her caring for her partner.

1. It adds great variety to the possible positions for orgasm.
2. It can be exciting to the woman to be able to actually taste her lover.
3. It is a clean activity, not messy.
4. It can be performed almost anywhere on very short notice. All it takes is unzipping and letting it fly. It allows for a great deal of imagination in terms of where it can be done: the office supply room, a shower, a coat closet, or an upstairs bedroom during a party. This can be risky, but for many partners, **the slight risk of being caught adds to the excitement.**
5. It is a wonderful way of stimulating a man who may be too tired or distracted to otherwise become aroused enough to get hard. It's easy and fun to suck a soft penis as well, and the man will frequently find he can develop an erection from fellatio easier than in any other way.

    Since it is difficult and often impossible to put a soft penis in a vagina and keep it there, with oral sex a woman can take a soft penis in her mouth, play with it, and thus take performance anxiety out of her lover's mind. Instead, she offers emotional and sexual support and receptiveness and with no orgasmic objective. Whether he comes or not doesn't matter. They are both going to have a good time, and he will appreciate the devoted attention.

    It's important to let your lover know that you delight in his penis whether it is soft or hard, because not being able to get hard when he expects to, or is expected to, can be a great ego shock for a man and extremely embarrassing. Since many men feel a soft penis is useless as a sexual tool, you can polish up his battered ego and show him that simply isn't true. There's lots you can do with it and a lot left to do in loving.

Many medications, oral pills, urethral inserts, and penile injections are available for those men who have persistent trouble getting erections. Now there is Viagra, the new pill that enhances erections in thirty to sixty minutes by allowing the blood to flow into the penis while keeping the veins shut tight so it can't flow out again. Since such easy, nonsurgical treatment is now available, a man should see a doctor if erection failure occurs regularly.

The Eyes Have It

And remember, as in all sex, to try to maintain eye contact as much as possible. Of course, if your head is buried in his crotch, it may be difficult, but otherwise, whether you are kneeling in front of your standing lover, or sitting on the floor on a pillow in front of your lover, sitting in a chair or kneeling in bed between his legs, it is important to glance frequently at his eyes to communicate with your eyes the fact that your kisses and whatever else you are doing is a physical expression of your mental and spiritual love.

In fellatio, even though it is called a blow job, it is extremely important that you do not try to blow into the penis. Forcing air up the urethra and into the bladder can cause serious medical problems.

Unfortunately, we don't have a language to describe the beauty of this form of lovemaking, and certainly "going down on a woman," or giving a blow job suggest a coarseness and a crudeness far removed from the delicacy and delight this way of lovemaking can offer.

Deep Throating During Fellatio

For some women, the ordinary ways of licking and sucking her man's penis are not enough. She craves something more profound. She wants to make a stronger gesture of love and will try deep-throating. Deep-throating is when a woman puts her partner's penis down the back of her throat and into her esophagus. This can be done only after a considerable amount of time is spent learning how to suppress the gag reflex.

You can try to do it by practicing with a hot dog or banana and inserting it deeply into your mouth and down your throat.

In order to swallow a man's penis with this deep-throat technique, it is best to align yourself on your belly with your head between his legs and your feet toward his head. This allows the curved erect penis to naturally follow the contour of you mouth down the back of your throat alongside your tongue and down into your esophagus.

It is only with considerable effort that this can be accomplished by any woman. The size of the penis, mouth, and throat are a consideration. While some women may be able to perform this with a normal or smaller-size lover, many women will find it impossible with a man who has a larger penis.

Practice and motivation are the key. However, since the head of the penis is far more sensitive than the shaft and base, being able to do this is not necessarily more stimulating for the man.

Body Piercing

You may have noticed some women wearing small gold balls or gold loops in their navels, ears, eyebrows, and elsewhere.

Nipple, clitoris, labia, navel, eyebrow piercing, and all the rest of this current fad have absolutely no erotic advantage. As a matter of fact, it may be dangerous and risky for several medical reasons including infection, transmission of HIV, and long-term pain.

As a physician, I therefore do not recommend it. In order for sex to be really pleasurable, it must be safe.

The American Dental Association has recently passed a resolution opposing oral piercing, which it also considers unsafe.

Self-Stimulation During Fellatio

It is possible for a woman to reach down and stimulate herself while sucking her lover's penis by rubbing her clitoral area, her vulva, or by inserting her finger in her vagina. However, while some women like it, this is distracting for other women, and alternating who is active in making love and who is passive in receiving it may be preferable.

But in any form of fellatio, the man is usually quite eager to feel a tight massaging of his penis and may without thinking try to hurry things up by pressuring the woman to take his penis in her mouth, take it deeper, swallow it, or move faster or slower by grabbing her head and simply shoving her down on him.

This is to be avoided unless you want to close the shop down for good. No one likes to be forced to choke!

She shouldn't allow this. It is much more effective for the man to demonstrate with moans and groans, pelvic movements and words, and perhaps very gentle hand contact with her head what he wants her to do and what feels good at the moment. Biting hard is usually unpleasant to all men and suggests an aggressive sexuality that is not appropriate during fellatio.

So, when you are playful, remember, both of you should always be gentle, your words, actions, and eyes brimming with love, your hearts giving all, your inhibitions gone, buried forever where they belong, your free giving to and taking from each other overwhelming the moment.

Chapter 13

Playing with Food

Having become familiar with the taste of the vagina and penis both before and during orgasm and ejaculation, having gotten to know these most personal and private parts of each other's bodies in the most intimate ways, having mingled your minds and spirits, you might now enjoy the taste of just play.

Try playing with foods, those mouthwatering delicacies that can add fun and pleasure and keep sex from getting routine.

Everyone likes to eat. So think of what you do when you make love as being the basic sauce, and now let us add some spices to perk the appetite for what can be the most delirious and passionate part of our lives.

David's Dilemma

Nancy accompanied her boyfriend to a conference in Washington, D.C. During the trip they found time to spend a day in bed and David ordered room service, including a tray of fruits and desserts such as ice cream, chocolate cake, and grapes. After much play, he

144

inserted a large piece of chocolate cake into Nancy's vagina and then proceeded to have intercourse with her, smearing his penis with the delicious and gooey chocolate. The cake was, of course, high in sugar and it entered his urethra along with bacteria from the vagina.

Several days later, after returning from their trip, David visited his urologist with intense discomfort when urinating. His doctor diagnosed an infection of the prostate and treated him with antibiotics. The only prevention would have been a condom or not trying it at all. It is therefore essential to realize that though you should enjoy yourself, playing with vegetables, fruits, or other substances in the vagina, on the penis, or around the anus must be done with the utmost thoughtfulness and hygiene in order to avoid infection.

Playing with food internally in the vagina or rectum always has risks. You must be with a known partner, preferably in a long-term monogamous relationship. (See Chapter 17 for medical precautions.)

When playing with food on or in either the man or woman, it is important to urinate both before and after play to cleanse the urethra from any substances that may have entered it. It is also important to empty the rectum.

We all enjoy whipped cream, and it is one of the safer things we can use on the outside of the vagina, the vulva, and labia or, for that matter, anywhere on the female or male body. You can even squirt it into the vagina with relative safety. And men and women enjoy the thought of a dab of whipped cream at the end of their partner's nipples, which they can look forward to licking and sucking off at the end of a long day, if you greet him with *you* rather than the traditional martini, Scotch, or glass of wine.

Some couples choose grapes, which can be popped into the vagina easily, one at a time, in as much abundance as is pleasurable and comfortable. They are easy and fun for the man to remove with his fingers and eat or for you to push out one by one. Or long, thin cucumbers, carrots, or squash. Or maybe pure chocolate candies or banana. Or how about a chocolate sundae or banana split?

It must be something that can easily be rinsed or douched out, so honey, for example, would not be good. Instead, try anointing the labia and clitoris with confectioners' sugar, liquor, or champagne. (Be careful, the alcohol in liquor may burn.)

One patient I had told me about how exquisitely arousing the sensation of a whole raw egg being lightly rolled up and down her skin, was, then, as her lover brought her to the point of orgasm with his hand, at that very moment cracking the egg and dripping it over her clitoris and oozing it between her labia and down her crack. In her case the egg was broken on the kitchen counter while she was having sex on it. Very practical.

It felt *sooo* good, she asked her lover to smear the egg all around and in her as she continued to feel the pulsing of her multiple orgasms and he rubbed her belly and buttocks with what was left of the egg, still raw, now scrambled.

Pomegranates, for some, may be the sexiest fruit there is if very ripe and sweet. It is fun to pop open the sections, squeeze them over each other, let the juices drip, then lick your lover's body, breaking pieces to pop in each other's mouth along the way. And kissing . . .   If you want to have fun with food and your male lover, his penis seems designed for dipping. Try such tasty concoctions as jelly, chocolate syrup, butterscotch syrup, ice cream, whipped cream, maple syrup, or whatever turns you on. What could be more inviting than a chocolate-covered penis?

Allison's Chocolate Decadence

A longtime patient of mine and I were chatting casually one day after her annual exam and she began to talk about anal sex, asking me if it was all right to try. When I assured her it was, she then told me the following story.

"You know, doctor, I would never in a million years think of touching that part of my husband. I had always thought of it as dirty and not the least bit sexy. But one evening he had a bit of a backache and I suggested he take a hot bath. He did, and I had fun washing him while he lay back, enjoying being helpless.

"Well, doctor, the flip side of the aggressive male just wants everything done for him. So I had fun spoiling him and then we both went to bed. As I was playing with his penis and sucking it, he smelled so good and was so clean, I suddenly, on dumb impulse, just reached for one of those small chocolates we keep near the bed for midnight snacking, and I stuck it against his anus.

"It began to melt from the heat of his body, and loving chocolate as I do, I suddenly grabbed his buttocks and began to lick and slurp ferociously at that melting chocolate blocking the hole to his anus. It tasted so fantastic. Not just the chocolate, but his warm body. That part of it between my lips, my tongue going back and forth and around in circles, and inhaling and sucking and drinking in the dripping, melting chocolate. It was fantastic.

"He began to groan with pleasure. I enjoyed the whole damn thing. I know it isn't just because I'm a chocoholic. I just enjoyed giving pleasure to a part of him that was strange and new to me. Doctor, I loved it. It opened a whole new world. Am I crazy?"

I assured her she wasn't and encouraged her to try variations, even to try inserting things in the anus such as grapes or M&Ms, being sure always that the lower bowel is clear of stool, which should be taken care of before lovemaking sessions anyway.

I do want to stress that putting candy, chocolate, or M&Ms into the anus is fine. The anus can basically have almost anything put in it from soup to nuts and really not develop any problems. The vagina, however, is quite another matter. Candy, syrups, and certain foods can alter the acid environment of the vagina and leave fragments of sugar and particles of food behind that can be either irritating or induce infection.

A Note of Caution

If you are going to play that way with food, you have to be prepared to take the consequences in terms of possibly developing a yeast infection, which is characterized by a thick, white, curdy, itchy discharge but is readily treatable with over-the-counter anti-yeast preparations. Food from the anus may transmit parasites or bacteria if your partner has an infection.

It is important when you are finished playing with food for the woman to use a vinegar douche (two tablespoons of white vinegar in a quart of water) to wash out any food that remains and to restore the normal vaginal acidity, which is necessary to inhibit the growth of bacteria and other germs.

If you don't want to bother making your own douche, disposable varieties such as a ready-to-use vinegar douche are very inexpensive and easy to handle, with each small squeeze bottle holding only the amount you will need for one time. Always be sure to let the water run in and out freely, removing all remaining food remnants and be careful *not* to press the lips of the vagina around the nozzle of the douche bag, because this increases the pressure of the fluid in the vagina and may force it up into the cervix, uterine cavity, and fallopian tubes, carrying with it bacteria that can cause pelvic infection, infertility, and chronic pelvic pain. However, if you are cautious, you should have a lot of fun.

Chapter 14

Controlling Ejaculation
and Building
Your Love Muscles
for Super Sex

To Rise or Not to Rise, That Is the Question

Most men have tried to force their ejaculation at one time or another or tried to get hard when they couldn't. Sometimes even with masturbation there are moments when a man can't come, much as he might want to.

Instead of accepting this, he tries to force an erection or ejaculation, rubbing and pulling and yanking himself vigorously until he finally is able to come, or he fails and gives up. This is detrimental to his physical, spiritual, and mental well-being. It probably lowers resistance to disease by causing stress, which reduces vitality and the immune protective response.

There are any number of reasons a man may not be able to get an erection or ejaculate. He may be stressed by circumstances at work. Or he may be physically exhausted, ill, or on medication or drugs that depress his normal functions. He may have had too long a lovemaking session, too much to drink, or be distracted by pressures such as the stock market's ups and downs, money, job, etc.

Probably the least likely causes are physical and psychological problems that require immediate medical attention or therapy.

Whatever the reason, when the mind is willing but the body is unforgiving, if he is unable to get an erection or ejaculate when he wishes or expects to, or thinks his lover expects him to, he should just relax and allow his energies to build. He should enjoy sex play without trying to prove himself.

His partner should be extremely sensitive to his predicament and should be loving, supportive, and nondemanding. She may entertain him and relieve the pressure by giving him a dose of fellatio. Or she could stimulate his senses by masturbating in front of him. In no case should she feel, or be made to feel, responsible.

WE ARE EACH RESPONSIBLE FOR OUR OWN ORGASMS.

Some women have the misguided idea that they are doing their lover a favor by helping to force or pressure him when he is having difficulty. This isn't so.

There are four rules men should remember:

1. Never force an erection.
2. Never force an ejaculation.
3. Never stop an ejaculation once it has started.
4. You are responsible for your own ejaculation.

Controlling Ejaculation

As I have pointed out, most of us, especially men, believe the whole purpose of sex is ejaculation. Many women also believe this and think their job is done once their lover ejaculates. Too often the woman prefers this to happen sooner rather than later. Since women need longer than men to reach the point of arousal where they can have an orgasm, they frequently feel under pressure, especially if there has not been sufficient foreplay. They are apt to think that it is taking them too long and the man will grow weary or bored trying to excite them and having to wait for them to orgasm.

Some men consciously hold off having their orgasm in order to spend the tender time necessary to arouse their partner with titillating foreplay so she can have an orgasm—and only after she comes does he come. This is an especially good technique late at night, when a man is likely to become drained of the vital energy necessary to enthusiastically continue for very long. He is weary and exhausted, she is aroused and frustrated. It is better to plan on her coming first to be fair and to keep both partners equally satisfied.

Sometimes after waiting a reasonable amount of time, with each trying hard to do what usually excites them, some women who simply can't get excited enough to make anything happen will finally give up, scream loudly, or moan softly and fake the whole thing.

Unfortunately, in the ritual of lovemaking, men's urgent physical demands to ejaculate sabotage intimacy and spiritual connection and fail to create a conscious harmony on the deeper level, which encourages sex and love to thrive. It is important, therefore, in order to have extraordinary sex, to achieve any stamina at all, and to prolong the length and depth of the love act, that the male partner learn ejaculatory control.

A boy in his teens learns to masturbate to orgasm without much trouble and isn't particularly exhausted at the conclusion. However, as a man ages, his sexual energies diminish somewhat and it takes longer to get an erection, longer to reach an orgasm, the force and volume of ejaculation may be less than they used to be, and after the man has finally come, the time that must pass (the so-called refractory period) before he can get hard or ejaculate again increases.

Stopping smoking (increasing oxygen in your body necessary for vigorous activity), exercising (increasing physical stamina), and hormone replacement (DHEA, testosterone, and growth hormone) all may help.

However, most important, I believe these effects of aging can be completely eradicated by the man who learns to gain conscious

control of his ejaculation and orgasm. You have heard and probably experienced ejaculatory control by forstalling your orgasm and maintaining the stimulation necessary for prolonged loving sex. What I discuss in this chapter is a new concept for many: that men can learn to have orgasms without ejaculating.

Remember that for both men and women, an orgasm is the *internal* experience of the explosive sexual climax perceived in the mind. Ejaculation is the *external* expression of this experience by the letting go of seminal fluids by the male and vaginal secretion and/or urine by the female.

Control allows the man to separate orgasm from ejaculation. It allows him to keep his orgasm inside his mind and body at will.

He learns how to extend his orgasms and make them last for many minutes, and in so doing, he can enjoy and assimilate a much higher degree of energy from his lover than he would experience from an immediately released ejaculation. He achieves the ability to establish a choice about whether or not to ejaculate. He will be in charge. It is thus very empowering for a man and may influence all aspects of his life by increasing his self-confidence.

To achieve control, the man needs first to become sensitive to his normal sexual response pattern. He usually experiences this in five phases:

1. **Arousal**—gets an erection, anticipates orgasm.
2. **Plateau**—arousal that remains at a relatively constant level until further stimulation increases pleasure to a higher step or plateau, or to orgasm. With control the man or woman may last through many increasingly intense sensory plateaus until orgasm is released.
3. **Orgasm**—a spontaneous, seizurelike spread of electrical and spiritual energy throughout the body along with involuntary spasms of the Love Muscles as well as most of the body. This may or may not be accompanied by ejaculation.
4. **Ejaculation** of seminal fluid mixed with sperm.

5. **Refractory period** after orgasm with ejaculation when the man is insensitive to further stimulation or may be hypersensitive, so continued stimulation is irritating. This period is absent or much shorter in orgasm without ejaculation.

I cannot predict how long a man will be able to sustain active intimacy, riding arousal to the edge of orgasm, and orgasm to the edge of ejaculation, reaching higher and higher plateaus each time, but I can predict with confidence that he will get better with practice, and that by rerouting his sexual energy in these ways, he will not only extend his lovemaking ability but, also, he and his partner will enjoy a much deeper experience than ever before in loving.

Each man has to discover his own formula for how often he releases his ejaculate. Some men prefer three or four times a week or more. Others may wish to ejaculate daily or several times a day. Still others find themselves feeling elated and satiated with more frequent orgasms and less frequent ejaculation. Like all sexual preferences, these choices may vary with time, experience, and partners.

Simple Techniques That Stop Ejaculation

There are three simple techniques that can be used without practice or training to stop ejaculation.

1. The Squeeze Technique

the female partner squeezes the penis from front to back with her fingertips to prevent ejaculation. She squeezes the head of the penis about an inch from the tip. The head of the penis is extremely sensitive, and if you squeeze the base of the head, it should respond in seconds as though you were flipping off a circuit breaker. The erection is temporarily wilted, and the desire for orgasm diminished, but both will return within a few minutes of resumed lovemaking.

2. The Pull Technique

in this technique the man or woman gently pulls down and squeezes the scrotum, holding for ten to thirty seconds. Be careful not to squeeze the testicles (*ouch*), but just above them, where the sac hangs from the body.

This can be a very discreet gesture that the man does himself or the woman does as she caresses his scrotum. This techniques assures that the man will not ejaculate and at the same time it allows him to stay inside the woman though with a softer erection.

3. The Press Technique

this is applied to the spot located halfway between the scrotum and the anus. This area overlies the back of the "missing third of the penis." During lovemaking, these three inches of "missing" penis respond just like the rest of the penis. They swell and become hard and are extremely sensitive to manipulation. You can feel it under the skin, and if the man squeezes his Love Muscles, you can see the direct connection between the penis, right through and under the scrotum and testicles, all the way to the rectum. (See diagram.)

Light stroking, touching, kissing, and sucking in this area is very stimulating for both sexes, and more so, the more sensitive the area becomes with Love Muscle awareness and development. However, if sudden firm pressure is applied to this spot it will turn around the direction of ejaculatory energy in a few seconds. Either partner may use his or her index and middle fingers to apply strong, constant pressure to this area. As you become proficient at it, the amount of pressure needed to forestall ejaculation becomes less and less.

Breath Control

Breath control is another element in the ability to control orgasm. Respiration and the pulse rate increase as the excitement of an orgasm is about to burst forth. Consciously slowing and deepening the breath as both partners **synchronize their breathing,** remain very still and connect with their eyes, the man clenching his Love Muscles, the woman relaxing hers, will aid his ability to control his orgasm and ejaculation.

It is said that breath is life.

I say, breathe together for love.

Breath control is an important aspect of sex. It is intimately associated with our level of emotional as well as physical arousal and stimulation.

In the realm of sex, one of the more threatening things men have to deal with is premature ejaculation. In learning to handle this problem breath control is exceedingly important. Regulate your breathing by slowing down the rate simultaneously with your partner and perhaps even with her taking a little of the lead, as she encourages you. By taking this simple step, you will notice that you gradually become more and more comfortable and have a greatly reduced sense of urgency with regard to impending ejaculation.

If you try breathing together slowly and deeply, telling yourself to relax with each breath, and at the same time using your Love Muscles to contract and restrain your orgasm, you will find a comfortable state of pleasure where you will remain aroused and experience an extremely high level of stimulation *without* ejaculation.

Match the rhythm of your breathing with the mesmerizing intensity of your loving gaze. Look deeply through the window of each other's eyes into each other's hearts and souls. It is an extremely intimate experience, creates new bonds, and reinforces your affection as lovers. Together you work to help give the man the power to stall his orgasm for the moment, then for several moments, then until he chooses.

Combining breath control with the simple techniques that stop ejaculation is a step toward sexual mastery that allows a man to extend lovemaking and gain the ability to choose the timing of his orgasms.

Finding Your Love Muscles

One of the crucial and more sophisticated methods for learning control of your orgasms is Love Muscle training. Many of us have some experience with personal trainers in gyms and clubs. But never has a personal trainer taught us how to build our Love Muscles. How many of you even realized you had such muscles?

Most of us can't picture what or where they are. (See diagrams in photo insert.) First you must identify them in your body, then strengthen and build them just as you would your biceps or leg muscles. Remember, the Love Muscles are in your pelvic and anal area. They are the major muscles of contraction in female as well as in male orgasm with, in the case of the male, the addition of the muscles surrounding the prostate gland. Better controlled muscles mean greater sensation for you and more enhanced sensation for your partner, since with more control, there are more ways for the woman to squeeze the man's penis and more ways for the man to bob or wriggle his penis inside her.

In women: The more tone you have in your Love Muscles, the more powerful your orgasm due to increased strength, duration, and number of muscle spasms per orgasm. Love Muscle toning means women more easily have multiple orgasms, and are more easily aroused to begin with (firm muscles transmit more sensation).

In men: Better controlled Love Muscles make for a strong, firm erection (coordinated Love Muscles squeeze more blood into the penis), increased strength, duration, and number of muscle spasms

per orgasm, and enable the man to separate orgasm from ejaculation. This allows men, like the women they love, to have multiple orgasms.

The way a man or woman can get a feeling for where these muscles are, is the next time you urinate, try to stop the flow by clenching. Or the next time you have a bowel movement, clench to stop it. The muscles you are using to accomplish this are your Love Muscles. They are an army of genital, vaginal, and anal muscles with fibers from several groups of pelvic muscles that surround, support, and contract together around the bladder, urethra, anus, rectum, and the lower third of the vagina in women, and the hidden third of the penis in men.

A popular misconception is that the pubococcygeus (PC) muscle is the only muscle involved in sex. This is anatomically and medically incorrect. When you read "PC muscle control," etc. in popular literature, translate PC to Love Muscles and you will have the right description for the *group* of muscles that are employed in love play and orgasm. (See diagrams in photo insert.)

Once a man has developed Love Muscle control, he has taken a giant step toward control of his ejaculation, for as soon as he begins to experience an impending orgasm, he can clench and hold his Love Muscles in a sustained contraction, which will reverse the flow of sexual energy.

Try it the next time you make love. As soon as the man starts to feel his orgasm arriving, both partners should stop all movement and the man should focus attention on his Love Muscles, clenching and holding them.

He should remain still, his Love Muscles clenched, and focus on his breathing as previously described. The rapid, panting of sexual arousal should be consciously slowed to regular deep breathing and should be helped along by the female. She should breathe slowly in unison with her partner and completely relax her Love Muscles until his feeling of urgency has passed.

Breath in the intention to relax.

Breathe out the urgency to ejaculate.

The man should not worry about the slight diminution of his erection, which can be up to twenty percent. This is bound to occur.

However, with resumed stimulation and activity, and the continued excitement of lovemaking, his erection will soon return and should be even stronger than before. Men will discover with Love Muscle control that their level of passion increases, their erections last longer, and the quality of their lovemaking is enriched.

Once you've identified the muscles by stopping your urine stream, if you're not too shy it is perfectly alright to try one of the following techniques to reinforce your findings. After a bowel movement, put a lubricated finger into your anus and squeeze hard if you are a man, or if you are a woman, place two fingers into your vagina and spread them as wide apart with as much strength as you can. Then try to squeeze them together using your muscles.

Now you have learned and verified what the Love Muscles really are. Also, if you are a man, try placing your finger behind and between the testicles and feel these muscles contract.

As a matter of fact, squeezing and relaxing the Love Muscles will make the man's erection bob up and down when he is lying on his back or standing.

Exercises for Gaining Love Muscle Awareness and Voluntary Control

Men and women should try the following exercises to learn to control their Love Muscles. Contract the muscles and hold for a count of three, then relax.

SQUEEZE—1—2—3.

RELAX.

REPEAT—ten times in a row, three times a day.

This simple exercise is known as the Kegel exercise for women. I call it the "Pelvic Crunch" for men. The exercise can be done while

reading, sitting in a car at a stoplight, on an airplane, in a restau-
rant, or an elevator, to distract yourself during a long, tedious
meeting, or just about anywhere at any time. After twenty-one days
it will result in a tremendous increase in your awareness of the
voluntary nature of these muscles and your ability to direct them.
So, if you see someone looking glassy-eyed and dreamily staring
into space, they may well be doing just this: squeezing those Love
Muscles!

It is also important to begin to lengthen the time you squeeze
your muscles. After doing it three times a day, squeezing for three
seconds each time, extend the squeezing to five seconds, seven seconds, ten seconds each time . . . as long as you can go. The more
you practice, the more aware you will become of your voluntary
control of these muscles.

Kegel suggested years ago that this exercise of the muscles could
help reduce involuntary urine leakage (stress urinary incontinence,
SUI) associated with coughing, laughing, and sneezing in women
whose bladder muscles had been weakened as a result of stretching
in childbirth.

Since Kegel exercises are performed without resistance, doing
them is like trying to strengthen your biceps by doing arm curls
without dumbbells. In the hundreds of patients for whom I prescribed this nonsurgical alternative for six to twelve months or
longer, I rarely noted enough significant increase in muscle strength
to avoid surgery. Usually there was only minimal decrease of involuntary urine loss.

Because Kegel exercises alone do not significantly strengthen the
component of the Love Muscles that is responsible for urinary continence, I suspect any improvement attributable to this exercise was
the result of enhancing the patient's awareness of the voluntary
nature of contracting the Love Muscles surrounding the bladder,
vaginal entrance, and anus (which means more muscle control).
This exercise probably never did make a *major* difference in muscle
mass, firmness, strength, or resting tone.

Anytime you repeat a muscle exercise, the neuromuscular wiring to that group gets enhanced. For example, if you start playing the piano, the more you practice, the more accurate and agile your fingers become, though they don't necessarily get any stronger. However, exercise *with* resistance does create significantly better muscle firmness, strength, tone, and consequently endurance.

Both Kegel and vaginal resistance exercises cause repetitive flexing and relaxing of the Love Muscle group, including the components that surround the bladder and contribute to urinary continence. Unfortunately, since Kegel exercises have never clinically increased, in my observation as a physician, the strength of those muscles (as a treatment for SUI) I came to the conclusion years ago that I wanted to invent a vaginal muscle exerciser to work these muscles against resistance. Treating SUI is one medical benefit. But there are numerous other health benefits.

Health Benefits

When you exercise your Love Muscles against resistance, you create many other advantages. Controlling the Love Muscles improves your health by giving you prolonged intimacy due to sexual strength and stamina. Uncontrolled weak Love Muscles allow the bladder and uterus to drop, which can cause chronic tension, lower backache and pain, or loss of protection to these organs during intercourse. The uterus and cervix may drop into the vagina almost to the point of coming out (called uterine prolapse), certainly to the position where jarring by the deeply penetrating penis during intercourse causes occasional pain.

Well-toned Love Muscles improve circulation to the genital organs, bladder, and uterus. They may indirectly prevent disease by increasing the flow of white blood cells, which defend the body against bacteria and viruses increasing the elimination of cellular metabolic waste, and increasing local bathing of cells in health-promoting oxygen and rejuvenating circulating hormones. These all contribute to the retardation of hormone-dependent aging, more youthful skin, and improved genital tone.

The Sexual Benefit

When you exercise a muscle against resistance, you also improve your sexuality in multiple ways:

1. You increase the resting tone of your muscles so that instead of being flabby, soft, and cushioning a touch, they are firm and have a tension that transmits a touch much more intensely. All touching sensations are stronger, more vivid, more clear, more exciting, and more titillating because there is literally more electrical energy coming out of those nerves.

2. You develop strength, mass, and endurance, which contributes to having more powerful orgasms. The muscles contract more strongly because they *are* stronger. So the perception of forceful orgasms is heightened enormously. Not only that, stronger muscles affect how long the orgasm lasts because the muscles don't fatigue as easily and thus the numbers of spasms per orgasm increases.

3. Because of your Love Muscle strength, you can clench your muscles and forestall an impending orgasm. Thus both women and men can reverse the flow of energy temporarily, and then be stimulated again and again to build up more and more powerful multiple orgasms. Strengthening these muscles creates the ability to control the timing of orgasms *by choice.*

A New Invention

Since it is really important to exercise all the muscles involved in the orgasmic spasm against progressive resistance, both for health and sexual advantages, I have finally done what I planned years ago. I have invented a revolutionary, safe, simple, easy-to-use new product for women called GyneFlex. It provides vaginal muscle exercise against resistance involving the *entire* Love Muscle group, and is of great benefit to all women.

GyneFlex may be used safely and with confidence that you will achieve results. However, if you wish medical supervision, check with your gynecologist.

For most men, whose Love Muscles are naturally tighter and stronger (including anal sphincter muscles), Love Muscle control and strength can be readily achieved from "Pelvic Crunch" workouts.

Since the male anatomy is different, squeezing/relaxing exercises when practiced to the point of becoming second nature are sufficient to develop enhanced orgasms, multiple orgasms, and voluntary control over ejaculation.

Summary of GyneFlex Exercise for Women

1. It treats the medical condition of stress urinary incontinence (SUI) and may cure it.
2. Use of **GyneFlex** makes Kegel exercises unnecessary. Result of regular daily exercise are generally obvious and documentable yourself in three weeks using the two-fingers-spread-apart technique.
3. It increases the sensitivity and heightens the mental perception of arousal of genital touching because of increased awareness of sensation.
4. How you perceive the quality of your orgasm is equal to the **number** of Love Muscle contractions (which determines the length of time of your orgasm) and the **strength** of Love Muscle contractions (which determine the intensity of feeling). Both are increased!
5. Because you can now remain aroused yet forestall or time your orgasms (in a variety of ways), the length

of time for reciprocal, intimate, and healing energy exchange is increased *enormously*.

6.   You can learn to sequentially contract your Love Muscles to play your lover's penis like a flute.

7.   You can draw your lover's penis deep inside by muscle control alone.

8.   Exercising any muscle increases blood flow into that area. Each of us has felt the tingling warmth resulting from vigorous exercise or deep massage. Increased pelvic blood flow helps eliminate metabolic toxins and may reduce the risk of minor genital infection.

Summary of Pelvic Crunch Exercise for Men

1.   It increases the sensitivity and heightens the mental perception of arousal from genital touching because of increased awareness of sensation.

2.   You will maintain firmer, stronger erections due to increased muscle control squeezing increased blood flow into your erect penis.

3.   How you perceive the quality or your orgasm is equal to the **number** of Love Muscle contractions, which determines the length of time of your orgasm, and the **strength** of Love Muscle contractions, which determine the intensity of feeling. Both are increased!

4.   Because you can now remain aroused yet forestall or time your orgasms (in a variety of ways), the length of time for reciprocal, intimate, and healing energy exchange is increased *enormously*.

5.   Because you can have orgasms without ejaculation, you can become a multiorgasmic lover.

6.   Exercising any muscle increases blood flow into that area. Each of us felt the tingling warmth resulting from vigorous exercise or deep massage. Increased pelvic blood flow helps eliminate metabolic toxins,

reduces the local accumulation of free radicals, and
may reduce the risk of minor genital and prostate
infection.

Advantages of Ejaculatory Control for the Man

When a man learns the techniques for controlling his ejaculate and
being able to have an orgasm without it, he is able to make love for
as long as he chooses. Longer periods of lovemaking mean more
intimate sexual play, more time for communication through intercourse, more of those electric feelings of arousal and desire, sensitivity and pleasure. This staying power is particularly meaningful because it encourages and extends the spiritual and mental sharing of
the sexual encounter.

The longer a man engages in lovemaking, the greater the buildup
of sexual tension and energy and the more powerful his orgasms.
When a man chooses to come (orgasm without ejaculation) after an
extended lovemaking session, his orgasm is far more explosive than
it otherwise would have been. In addition, the recovery period
between erections is very short since he hasn't spent his sexual
energyon ejaculation. He has energy on reserve and therefore his
continuing interest in loving builds.

And so, with nonejaculation orgasms, the man doesn't feel physically wasted as he does from ejaculation. Therefore he won't shut
down physically, mentally, and emotionally after sex. This can be of
great importance to the woman, who is often frustrated by the sudden withdrawal of her partner and the loss of both his erection and
his interest when she hasn't had an orgasm herself.

Even when both do experience orgasms, his shutting down after
ejaculation can be disappointing to her because her orgasm has left
her with lots of energy and she may want to continue to be intimate, while he is about as relaxed as he ever gets. So relaxed, in
fact, that the next step may be snoring sleep rather than soaring sex.

Advantages of Control for the Woman

Even more significant for extended lovemaking than the ability the man achieves with control of his ejaculation is the potential for his lover. The man who is not rushed in loving and who has no personal, immediate ejaculation intent lurking in the shadows of his consciousness is able to love and experience the act of sex differently.

His lovemaking becomes far more loving because it has less to do with reaching orgasm, and more to do with pleasure freely given.

This is the opposite of a man in the habit of taking sex from a woman, using her, and giving nothing back. The woman who has been thus abused by men will now find she is able to rekindle her ability to love and feel it with unequaled depth, knowing that this "new" man is giving his love with all his heart and asking nothing in return, no obligation to help him ejaculate.

The man who is capable of this kind of sexual control seems to give the woman not only his love, seen in unselfish splendor, but freedom.

This is *the freedom to finally lose control of herself,* which is the single most important element in her being able to have one or more fantastic orgasms.

It builds the trust necessary for his woman to slip temporarily out of herself and give up control. *Her* orgasmic potential increases with *his* discipline. She doesn't feel pressured. And it's a great thing for a man to feel he can influence his woman's orgasm. It does wonders for his own ego and self-worth.

Having orgasmic control is the single most important step in elevating sex to art.

If practiced for a few minutes a day, these exercises have a profound effect on lovemaking. Within three weeks of daily practice, a woman will be able to play with her lover's penis with her vaginal muscles.

Advanced lovers learn to combine Love Muscle contraction with techniques of touching and massaging the clitoris, penis, and anus that take them to previously unimagined levels of excitement and arousal.

Since clenching the Love Muscles against resistance, holding, then releasing will build muscle control, the woman can voluntarily clench and hold the penis as many times during lovemaking as she wants.

These clenching-releasing internal exercises can lead to some amazing tricks for the unending entertainment and pleasure of her lover. If she concentrates on her muscular contractions, she can learn to actually contract different layers of her Love Muscles in a ringlike fashion, contracting the outer ones first and then the inner ones while pulling her stomach in so that it results in a sucking-in sensation of the penis into the vagina. (Remember the stories that Vietnam vets tell of working women being able to puff on cigarettes placed in their vaginas? This is how.)

The woman should visualize her vagina as a cylinder composed of rings or fingers closed in a loop. She then contracts her trained muscles as though squeezing her fingers, one after the other. When her Love Muscles are well-controlled, a woman can learn to manipulate them—outermost to innermost—so that the separate groups of muscle fibers can contract sequentially.

It is an art that results in a situation where the woman can play these rings of muscles as if they were separate notes in a musical composition. She can create cords, change keys, and compose refrains, and in doing so transmit a powerful, intimate symphony to her lover without even moving her body.

She can do this while sitting on top of him with her legs wrapped behind him while he is sitting with his legs crossed as though meditating, or while lying on his back in bed. The man, too, can at the same time contract his Love Muscles and produce a bobbing, pulsating motion inside her as the two lovers create incredible sensations for each other without any external movement of the hips or body at all.

A woman who uses the contractions of her Love Muscles during intercourse voluntarily rather then waiting for those contractions to occur during orgasm, is able to pull her lover's penis deeper and deeper inside her. If these contractions are performed as she inhales, and if she holds her breath as long as she can, squeezing and bathing the penis in her energy, she then may release her contraction with exhilaration.

The man should inhale as the woman exhales, visualizing her energy, which he draws up into himself. With this kind of loving, the penis penetrates deep inside the vagina, the nipples of both partners are pressed firmly together, the man breathes out, conscious of his own energy and visualizing his penis growing, lengthening, and thickening inside his partner. The woman breathes in as he breathes out, conscious of receiving his energy, visualizing her vagina as drawing his penis into her as she controls her Love Muscles, her breathing, and gazes deeply and lovingly into his eyes.

Thus both partners give each other vital energy in this warm and exquisite form of loving. Of course a woman can perform Love Muscle control alone. However, when the man joins her because he has trained his own Love Muscles and learned ejaculatory control, he is an active participant in one of the most intimate and spiritually connected forms of lovemaking.

Chapter 15

Love Toys

Toys are one of the first things you learn about as a baby. You play with them for relaxation and amusement until you are older, when you stuff them away in an attic or basement and switch to hobbies and sports. Toys are for children. Right? Wrong.

When used for adult sex play, toys can revolutionize your style of lovemaking, your enjoyment, and the quality of orgasm you have. I use a strong word like revolutionize because I mean just that. Once you have learned to enjoy sex toys, your life will never again be the same.

Now, if you are like many people, you will be shocked. SEX TOYS? Aren't they dirty, vulgar, and obscene, and not for women or men with any class, style, or elegance? Surely *nice* people would never be seen in one of those adult toy stores.

Well, wrong again.

With the increasing openness to sexual knowledge and women's health, it is amazing how many women have bought sex toys such as vibrators and dildos and are using them with and without their male partners, even though their friends may not know it.

In fact, I was surprised to see that America's celebrity sex counselor, Dr. Ruth Westheimer, is advertising an adult sex toy called the Eroscillator, which has sideways movement. She calls it an aid to "achieve faster, easier, better orgasms." Well, if Dr. Ruth says toys are okay, they're got to be *okay*.

Sexual love, enhanced by toys, can be the ultimate antidote to stress.

The Case of Lois

During one of her annual checkups, Lois told me about the difficulty she was having reaching orgasm.

"I used to have sex frequently when I was first married and had no trouble reaching an orgasm," she explained, "and a good one at that. Then, as I grew older—you know I'm in my fifties now—I had more and more trouble.

"About this time I was divorced, and although alone, I still had sex urges and wanted to have orgasms, which I had always enjoyed. So, when I went to bed at night, and was really in the mood, I'd turn on my belly, my favorite position when I used to masturbate, and I'd play with myself.

"I'd try to think of a fantasy that had always excited me, and I'd play with myself—and play, and play and massage and push, and massage and press and wiggle back and forth—until I began to wet the sheets with sweat and my fingers ached with tension and I could hardly move them. Yet nothing happened. Literally hours went by. Can you imagine? I played with myself for two hours on the clock until I finally gave up.

"I began to think I was too old to have an orgasm and was at the point of believing I had entered old age until one day a close male friend suggested I buy a vibrator. I was shocked and nearly decided to stop seeing him. I thought it was a vulgar thing to do. Certainly it was obscene, like those magazines filled with pornography that are mailed in brown paper wrappers.

"Then a funny thing happened. I was at my ex-husband's house. He's a rather important executive, very VIP, and I noticed a long pink plastic thing shaped a little bit like a penis lying on the night table and asked him what it was. He blushed, picked it up and tried to hide it, but when I insisted, he told me it was a vibrator his current girlfriend had left out.

"I have to admit the women I knew had never spoken about sex toys. I was sure none of them ever had used one, and I had never even seen one myself. So when he told me what it was, I asked him how it worked, and he quickly turned it on and off and even more quickly put it away.

"But you know, I couldn't help wondering if that plastic vibrator was the cause of his leaving me. Did he have better sex with *her* because of it? I'll never know.

"So one day my friend and I went to a sex shop, and totally embarrassed, I picked out a vibrator or two and something for lubrication. I took them home where I kept them in the paper bag on the floor of my closet. I was afraid to try them for months. I felt silly.

"Then one night when I was alone I felt that familiar urge. I hadn't had an orgasm in so long. So I got really brave and desperate and went to the bag in my closet, smeared one of the vibrators with lubricant, turned off all the lights, and took it to bed with me.

"I turned the switch to on and felt the thing vibrating like crazy in my hand. I got into my favorite position in bed, held it against my clitoris, and let it go to work. Doctor, would you believe— about five minutes later I had a whopping orgasm that sent me through the roof. Five minutes!

"That little vibrator seemed like it was shaking at about two thousand times a minute compared to the paltry vibrations that my poor stiff fingers could manage. It was amazing. So, now I'm young again and sexy and happy and healed. My skin really glows. I only wish I'd tried something like this with my ex-husband."

A Medical View

As a physician I recommend using a vibrator:

1. To help women have their first orgasm
2. To add variety and spice to lovemaking
3. To reduce depression and irritability
4. Before menstruating to aid blood flow and reduce menstrual cramps

Further, using vibrators and other toys (as well as having intercourse) during pregnancy is perfectly acceptable as long as you do not use a dildo vibrator with any force in the vagina, but, rather, use only external clitoral-vulvar stimulation. Women who have a history of premature labor or any indication their labor might start too early should not, during their last trimester of pregnancy, use vibrators on their bellies, backs, or genitals or have intercourse, because orgasms can cause the onset of labor.

Toys and Women's Lib

Some people not only think that well-brought-up women don't use toys, but many think they are demeaning to women. However, as early as the 1970s NOW held its first women's sexuality conference in New York and a NOW member started a mail-order business where women could shop for toys without embarrassment.

Some felt this was being a pro-sex feminist. It was emphasizing the importance of women's sexual liberation. However, not all feminists agree and others may have difficulty with this concept.

I don't see sex toys as any more objectionable than taking advantage of the automobile to cover a lot of ground rather than walking.

Walking is all right if that's what you want to do, but taking a car will get you much farther, faster. Or using a crutch to help you walk if you are crippled. If you are sexually shy, you need help. Often it is the only way a woman can experience an orgasm. If you are sexually adventurous, you desire more ways to have fun. And that is what sex toys are: aids to achieving pleasure and orgasms.

Because about a third of women do not have orgasms when they wish, toys are obviously something worth considering

Finding a Toy Source

Conquering any feelings of shyness or embarrassment, look in the yellow pages of your phone book under the heading "Novelties" or "Lingerie." You will find listings for adult toy stores. Go alone or with a friend. The salespeople are usually friendly, warm, understanding, and full of advice. They will even insert the batteries for you once you've chosen the toys you want to buy. Be sure to also buy a bottle of lubricant such as Astroglide.

If you keep your toys readily accessible *in the bedroom* and not hidden away somewhere, you are more likely to use them and incorporate them regularly into your love life. You may want to keep each one in a Ziploc plastic bag or plastic container, and they won't get all tangled up with one another when you put them away in your toy chest.

Toys to Play With

Toys are fine. Toys are fun. Toys are healthy. Toys are sexy. Toys are safe.

They offer a tremendous range of experience that could not otherwise be had. They add to what we are able to bring to our sexual encounters with our hands, mouths, lips, and bodies. Because of their incredible speed, they enable you to have a stronger orgasm and they are an advantage if there are time constraints. They add that extra stimulation to help you climax sooner.

Naturally, you will be hesitant about using toys at first. However, once you've actually tried one, you will never be shy again. Your newly discovered pleasure will overwhelm any shyness. And do not feel that the use of toys is habit forming. Toys will never substitute for the shared energy that mutual love provides.

Sex toys used alone in privacy is a form of masturbation.

Sex toys used in any way with your lover present is a way of sharing sex with your lover. Shared intimacy is the most available and natural aphrodisiac there is. Lovers get turned on watching or helping their partners play.

There is a vast variety of plug-in electric and battery-operated vibrators. They come in many types, sizes, and shapes.

Approach toys with the same attitude as you approach loving in general. With openness, curiosity, a sense of discovery, and a sense that everything is all right as long as it doesn't hurt.

You'll soon discover that certain things feel good sometimes and other things feel good at other times. Following is an overview. The rest is up to you.

Electric Vibrators

Toys that feel good most of the time are electric vibrators. These are strong, powerful, quiet, generally well made, and are historically marketed for the relief of muscular tension. An electric vibrator will last for years and it won't electrocute you as long as you don't take it into the bathtub or get it wet. It's well worth the investment and trouble of buying an extension cord. If you decide to use electric, plug-in models, the problem of batteries wearing out every twenty minutes or half hour, perhaps during a crucial moment, will be eliminated. However, since the wiring in most vibrating dildos is so cheap that strong alkaline batteries burn them up, always use regular ordinary batteries for your battery-powered toys and plan on replacing these frequently.

It is curious that the companies that manufacture the best plug-in vibrators for massage still can't bring themselves to admit the potential sexual applications of these products. It is as if they are embarrassed to acknowledge or advertise the possible sexual use of personal care products.

There are basically two types of electric plug-in vibrators, coil-operated and motor-operated. The coil model looks like a handheld hair dryer with the vibrating head at right angles to the handle. Inside, it has an electromagnetic coil, not a motor.

Coil-operated vibrators come with four to six plastic attachments of varying flexibility that fit on a vibrating post and are designed for different parts of the body. There are attachments specifically good for clitoral stimulation, some of which may be inserted into the vagina, and a twig type, which is designed for simultaneous stimulation of the clitoris and vagina. Some women rave about this, while others are unimpressed.

For men, there is a tulip-shaped attachment to a coil vibrator called a cup. I have not found any men who really enjoy it.

Vibrators with rheostats that adjust the speed do not offer a significant advantage over two-speed models, as one can vary the touch and firmness of pressure by simply pressing any vibrator more softly or harder.

The Magic Wand

The wand is a longer, motor-driven toy with different attachments available separately that fit on the end. Wand vibrators are slightly larger, slower, and noisier in comparison with coil-type vibrators. They have a ball-shaped soft head attached to a flexible neck, which connects to the vibrator body. Most are two-speed. These are the best.

Compared to coil-type vibrators, the wand's vibration is deeper and stronger and the relatively larger surface of the vibrating head spreads out the vibration, making the wand preferable for both massage and sexual use. Coil types produce a much smaller but faster vibration because the distance the head moves back and forth is much shorter.

For women who don't have orgasms, there is no doubt that the wand-type vibrator rather than the coil type is best for a first experience, though either type of vibrator does an adequate job.

The coil type's smaller size and silence have made some people feel this is better for use when two partners are playing together. But if the couple is in a face-to-face position, someone's hand has to be in between their bodies to hold the vibrator and to direct it.

The wand type's advantage is that a couple finds the ball-shaped attachment fits nicely between the two sets of genitals in many positions without holding it. Another advantage when couples use it is that if one or both people are new to vibrators, the vibrator can be used for massage until the person becomes comfortable with it.

Wand- and coil-type vibrators can overheat if they are left on for more than half an hour. Many people own more than one wand vibrator so they can let one cool off while they use their backup.

I do not recommend double-headed vibrators, as they are too awkward to be practical, though some people say they can be used on the clitoris and vulva or clitoris and anus simultaneously.

How to Use the Wand

Using a light lubricant like Astroglide to keep from rubbing your skin, I suggest that you hold your wand very lightly against the shaft of the clitoris. Vary the strokes. You can try a gentle kneading motion, then a kind of light tapping or brushing with it. Find out what feels good and where it feels best, which, of course, will change during different phases of stimulation. This vibrator is easiest to use with the woman lying on her back. Various attachments that fit snugly over the ball are available.

If you had to choose one vibrator that would be successful for most people, it would be a wand. If accidentally left out and discovered by curious eyes, it could easily pass as a massager for tired neck muscles.

The Butterfly

Another type of vibrator is called the butterfly. It fits over the clitoris and is usually battery operated, though I have seen plug-in models. This strap-on is capable of causing orgasmic clitoral stimulation, while by design allowing for simultaneous vaginal penetration with either another toy or the penis.

Eggs and Bullets

Some battery-powered vibrators are shaped like small eggs. There is now a longer one, about four inches, that is shaped like a bullet. Both the eggs and the bullet attach by a two-foot-long cord to a rheostat that controls speed. There is even a radio-controlled egg that is available.

Some women find the sensation of vibrating eggs inserted in the vagina pleasurable, but usually this is because the vibrations bring one's attention to focus on the pelvic area rather than on providing direct stimulation. The eggs do not stimulate the G-spot and should not be left in for prolonged periods.

There is a new variety of egg called the Super Egg with a much more stable rheostat, which is attached to a microchip. This state-of-the-art egg is several times more expensive than the regular egg. However, the power unit unplugs easily from the electric cord and therefore it has many playful possibilities.

You can insert the egg and leave the cord discreetly placed but accessible to the man. Your man now carries the power supply and can plug you in and turn you on intermittently! This way of giving you pleasure is more teasing than sexually orgasmic and certainly is part of the playful attitude toward sex that I am trying to encourage as healthy.

Double bullets are small vibrating balls that are available for vaginal or anal stimulation in which two balls are connected to one speed control. These may be used with one in the vagina and one in the rectum of the female partner, or, for even more fun, try one in the vagina or rectum of the female and one in the rectum of the male partner.

When you turn yourself on, you are turning both of you on.

And even though the stimulation is not one that is likely to cause orgasm or ejaculation, it certainly is one that reminds both partners about their sexuality and focuses their attention on loving in a dramatic, exciting, and different way.

Dildos

A dildo is a cylinder vibrator that is shaped like an erect penis. Dildos also come in a variety of shapes and sizes, including curved models to reach your G-spot, and may be made of hard plastic, Lucite, rubber, vinyl, latex, or other materials. There are now quite soft, natural-feeling dildos, which are more expensive. Dildos are available anywhere from an inch and a half to two inches in width and from five inches to fifteen inches in length. Sometimes they come with veins or a foreskin in colors that imitate a penis realistically. Some are so enormous that they are intimidating and unreal, while others are so small they are extremely discreet and very practical.

You should try soft ones, hard ones, different size ones, waterproof ones, curved ones, whatever appeals to you. Most are battery operated, but recently some softer dildo-shaped vibrators have come out with electric plug-in models. In either case, you should choose a comfortable size to fit your vagina. Use it much the way you would the Magic Wand, rubbing it over the clitoris and the external part of your labia. Become familiar with the sensation. If it is no fun this time, put it away for another day.

When you decide to use it, the dildo should be clean and well lubricated with your own juices or Astroglide (or another water-soluble equivalent) before inserting it into your vagina. Avoid petroleum-based products like Vaseline, as they are sticky, don't wash off easily, generally unnecessary, and best reserved for anal ease. They also react unfavorably with condoms.

When it is inside your vagina, move the dildo around. Simply moving the dildo in and out does not put it in contact with the clitoris or G-spot area sufficiently to be particularly erotic. If it doesn't come into contact with the clitoris or the external areas that contain all the nerves, it is really in contact with nothing, since the deeper two thirds of the vagina is dilated or open during the arousal phase.

People who attempt to get much stimulation from dildo-shaped vibrators by simply inserting them and moving them in and out are going to spend more time exercising their arm and their minds than stimulating themselves or their partners.

As I have indicated, this vibrator is easy to use on the clitoris or to move around within the vagina, where it can be rubbed over the G-spot, but if it comes into contact with the cervix and uterus, and is jarred vigorously, it may cause pain. Therefore, gentle exploratory motions are best to start.

It is only when a separate toy or fingers are used to stimulate the clitoris that the dildo's presence in the vagina moving in and out starts to feel really good. Move the dildo in a circle at different levels of depth and notice what feels good and where. It can also be inserted anally. Actually, some women keep two, one for vaginal use, and a smaller one for anal use. They may even be safely used simultaneously.

The dildo has been around for many years in men's and women's

Love Muscles (blue) Viewed From Below

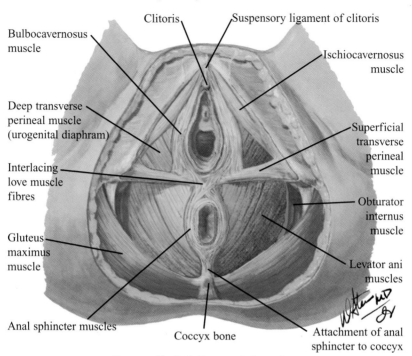

Clitoris

Suspensory ligament of clitoris

Bulbocavernosus muscle

Ischiocavernosus muscle

Deep transverse perineal muscle (urogenital diaphram)

Superficial transverse perineal muscle

Interlacing love muscle fibres

Obturator internus muscle

Gluteus maximus muscle

Levator ani muscles

Anal sphincter muscles

Coccyx bone

Attachment of anal sphincter to coccyx

Superficial Love Muscles

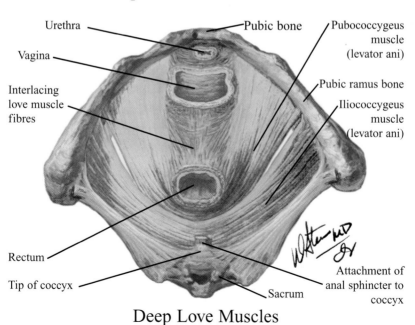

Urethra

Pubic bone

Pubococcygeus muscle (levator ani)

Vagina

Interlacing love muscle fibres

Pubic ramus bone

Iliococcygeus muscle (levator ani)

Rectum

Tip of coccyx

Sacrum

Attachment of anal sphincter to coccyx

Deep Love Muscles

Female Love Muscles (shown in blue)

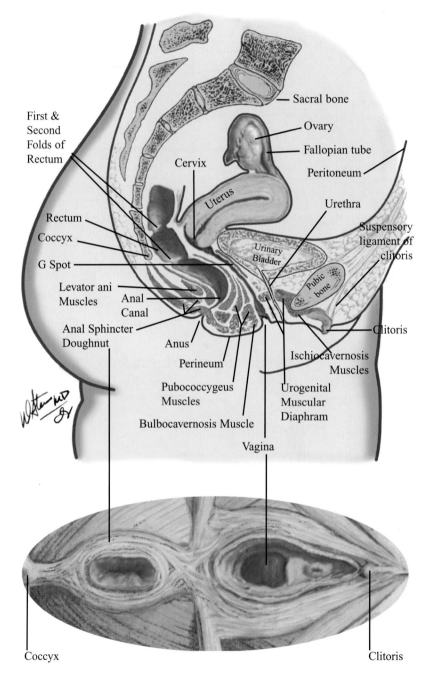

Sacral bone

First & Second Folds of Rectum

Ovary

Fallopian tube

Peritoneum

Cervix

Urethra

Uterus

Rectum

Suspensory ligament of clitoris

Coccyx

Urinary Bladder

G Spot

Pubic bone

Levator ani Muscles

Anal Canal

Anal Sphincter Doughnut

Anus

Clitoris

Perineum

Ischiocavernosis Muscles

Pubococcygeus Muscles

Urogenital Muscular Diaphram

Bulbocavernosis Muscle

Vagina

Coccyx

Clitoris

Detail of Female Love Muscles seen from below.

Male Love Muscles (shown in blue)

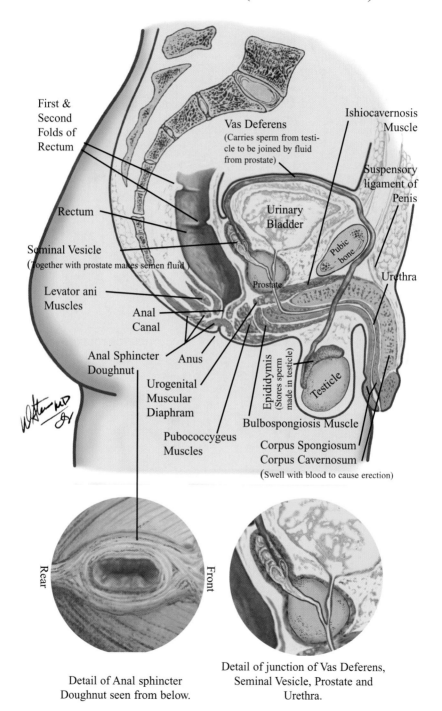

First & Second Folds of Rectum

Vas Deferens
(Carries sperm from testicle to be joined by fluid from prostate)

Ishiocavernosis Muscle

Suspensory ligament of Penis

Rectum

Urinary Bladder

Pubic bone

Seminal Vesicle
(Together with prostate makes semen fluid)

Prostate

Urethra

Levator ani Muscles

Anal Canal

Anal Sphincter Doughnut

Anus

Urogenital Muscular Diaphram

Epididymis
(Stores sperm made in testicle)

Testicle

Bulbospongiosis Muscle

Pubococcygeus Muscles

Corpus Spongiosum
Corpus Cavernosum
(Swell with blood to cause erection)

Rear

Front

Detail of Anal sphincter Doughnut seen from below.

Detail of junction of Vas Deferens, Seminal Vesicle, Prostate and Urethra.

GyneFlex Exerciser (Love Muscles Shown In Blue)

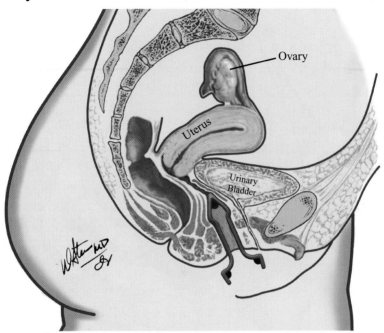

GyneFlex inserted in vagina: love muscles relaxed

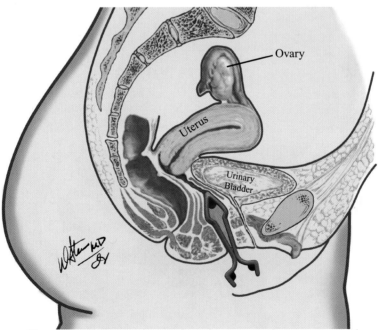

Gyneflex inserted in vagina: love muscles contracted

magazines, adult novelty stores, and catalogs. Unfortunately, because no instructions are packaged with this kind of vibrator, many a woman and her man have spent hours shoving the thing in and out of her vagina wondering how long the batteries will last and why she doesn't feel very much.

For most women, their sexual sensitivity is greatest on the clitoris, the G-spot, vulva, and the area between the vulva and the anus.

At the present time a vibrator that plugs into a car's cigarette lighter is available in a dildo shape. Since I was an advocate for seat-belt laws, I do not encourage people to play while driving. I mention this for possible use when parked.

Those who are given a vibrator by a well-intentioned partner frequently are given a dildo-shaped, hard plastic vibrator that they don't know what to do with and rarely are given a vibrator such as a Magic Wand or Pocket Rocket, which are easy to use by an inexperienced person.

The Pocket Rocket

This is a small vibrator that is battery operated. It's only about four inches long and an inch wide. It is easily transported in a pocket or purse and is primarily intended for clitoral stimulation, though it can be used around and in the vaginal entrance. There is a waterproof model now available called the Water Dancer which even comes with attachable soft and flexible "rabbit ears" for clitoral stimulation.

Many women find this a convenient toy to take with them when traveling or to use with their partner for spontaneous sex in a variety of locations. I suggest getting a waterproof one, which makes it easier to clean. It's also a good idea to get a backup, so if one breaks on a trip, you are not out of luck. It is a perfect substitute or addition to the Magic Wand.

Apollo Vibrator

This new variable-speed vibrator is made of PVC, which is nearly indestructible. It is more powerful than the Pocket Rocket since it uses two AA batteries instead of one. It is six inches long, shaped like a blunt-ended cigar, with one end wider and closer to the motor causing more intense vibrations. Its two ends snap together and break apart for battery change, hence its name.

Swedish Hand Vibrator

While the word "vibrator" conjures up a white, hard, plastic phallus, the word "massager" doesn't. I recently found a Swedish massager when cleaning out my mother's closet. It straps over the back of your hand and causes your hand to vibrate. This is the kind my grandmother also kept around to sooth irritated muscles.

My impression is that very few women have used this kind of vibrator for solo sex and that very few men have successfully used it to bring their partners to orgasm. The idea, of course, is that you touch your genitals with a warm, sensitive hand rather than hard, plastic or rubber. The vibrations are transferred through your hand and are relatively gentle.

The disadvantages are that these massagers are quite heavy, the vibrations shake your hand into numbness, and the springlike straps can catch pubic hair.

Ben-Wa Balls

These heavy-as-lead balls, neither electric nor battery powered, generally an inch to an inch and a half in diameter sometimes gold-plated, sometimes containing a ball bearing, are inserted in the vagina. Love Muscles are used to hold the balls in. The idea is that the movement of the balls inside can be felt by the women wearing them. Their weight requires tight Love Muscles to hold them in while walking or jogging (mentioned for thoroughness; they don't do much for most).

Finally, there is a chain of balls that vibrate at the same time that can be inserted into the vagina or rectum. These are usually not well constructed (be sure to use an emery board to file down the rough molding edges before inserting them) and are more of a curiosity than of practical benefit.

Pearl Rabbit and Princess Toys

One example of a terrific toy is the Pearl Rabbit. This is really two vibrators in one. A battery-operated motor rotates a phallic-shaped dildolike penis, and a separate motor causes a curved extension with very soft "rabbit" ears to vibrate. The "penis" fits into the vagina, of course, while the ears stimulate the clitoris at the same time. Some models have rotating balls the size of pearls (hence the name) on the base of the "penis," which rotate in the area of the vaginal Love Muscles to stimulate them as well. Rabbit-ear vibration, dildo rotation, and pearls turning, all respond to separate variable-speed rheostats.

Some women tell me the Pearl Rabbit gives them the most intense stimulation they have ever had and causes orgasms that are somewhere between fantastic and unbelievable. Most are made in China, not well constructed, and can't be counted on to last more than a dozen lovemaking sessions. A new and better model is made in Japan, has solid construction, and a durable state-of-the-art microchip for its advance rheostat. Called the Princess, it's the best, though quite expensive.

Double-Headed Toys

There are double-headed nonvibrating, soft latex toys designed to be inserted into the vaginas of two female lovers simultaneously, or one head into the vagina of the woman and the other head into the anus of her male lover, or each into the anuses of two male lovers. Since they don't vibrate, the movement is back and forth (in one and out of the other) and is dependent on body movement and hand control. They may be used together with other toys simultaneously for some really exotic sexual adventure.

Shower and Bath Toys

Lovers naturally enjoy playing with water . . . washing each other, bathing each other, even shaving each other. Many women find that masturbation is easily accomplished through the use of a shower with attached hose and adjustable nozzle. Others find that the water of a well-located Jacuzzi jet may serve double duty as a delightful and readily accessible water toy.

From a medical point of view, these are fine as long as the forceful stream of water is directed over the clitoris and vulva and not directly into the vagina. Recall that forceful injection of water into the vagina can carry bacteria through the cervix and up into the womb where serious infection is possible.

All waterproof (and therefore washable) toys may be used in the bath or Jacuzzi.

Anal Toys

There are many safe and fine ways to enjoy toys anally. Some, like anal beads, stimulate intense sensation at the very sensitive, doughnutlike anal sphincter. Others that probe deeper put pressure on as they slide back and forth over the prostate gland, enhancing a new internal arousal that is well worth discovering. The prostate gland and the anus are both erogenous zones of the highest order while the prostate responds to massage and movement, the rectum responds to distension, hence, the inflatable multi-speed vibrating plug stimulates both ways simultaneously. See Chapters 17 and 18 for further information.

Using a Vibrator—the Rules

When using a toy that vibrates, it is almost impossible for the man to know how hard he is pushing and exactly where he is pushing. The man must be careful not to cause discomfort, which can be distracting or painful.

Any way you use one, whether you use it on yourself or on your partner, whether you use it near the clitoris, on the clitoris, in the vagina, in the anus, around the anus, or just about anywhere, be sure and follow these rules:

1. If it hurts, STOP.
2. Do not use a vibrator on a raw or inflamed area.
3. Do not use a vibrator if you have a vaginal or bladder infection.
4. Never put a vibrator that has been in your anus into your vagina without washing it first.

Care of Your Toys

After use, wash your toys in lukewarm soapy water with a washcloth kept especially for this purpose. If you have lubricated them, you should use a dishwashing detergent that cuts grease. The important thing is that the detergent bottle say antibacterial and degreasing.

Be careful not to let water get into the battery or electrical components for obvious reasons. This is a near impossibility with many of the cheaper models currently available. After washing, dry them off with a towel. Then pour isopropyl alcohol over them. Leave the alcohol on them for a minute to be sure to kill any remaining germs, then rinse, dry, and put them away in your locked toy chest. If the toy is electrical, the cord should be cleaned with a damp washcloth and dried.

Your toys will last longer with this care and you will be much less likely to contract an infection. If you use the toys with more than one partner, you should put a condom on them to prevent passing bacteria back and forth between partners. And if you use battery toys, don't forget to keep a good supply of fresh batteries in your toy chest.

Towels

It seems that the more pleasurable lovemaking is the more messy it becomes. There are fragrant oils and creams you massage on your lover's body. There are also secretions that are part of loving itself. Whether they be vaginal or from a lubricant, you don't want a mess.

These substances will all leave marks and stain good linens and pretty sheets. Since it is nice to have attractive sheets, a special set of towels becomes a logical necessity. Rather than using your expensive towels, I suggest getting a fairly large collection of hand towels and larger bath towels that are plain white. This allows them to be washed with bleach and disinfected and also allows you to preserve your expensive towels for personal use and to keep them separate from your play towels. In addition to your white towels, you should have a supply of white washcloths that you can saturate in warm water after lovemaking to wash the genitals of your partner. This will not only clean the body, but the warm, fresh sensation is great.

This is all part of the general attitude of making love play easy, fun, and safe.

Toys Are Good

Toys are a healthy concept and are meant to bring happiness. They allow playful experimentation. They do not change the ways and places you like to be stimulated or keep you from trying something different.

So, here is a new toy. What can you do with it? Let's find out.

Playing with toys with your partner, if you have one, or alone, if you don't, opens the doors to new adventures for the rest of your life. It opens the doors because it opens your mind and changes your attitude. It is one way to become connected to the person you love, be they someone of the same sex or the opposite sex.

Toys are part of your sexual education. Like any education, you may not use what you learn for months or years.

It is all right to put it off for another day.

It is *not* all right to remain ignorant of the possibilities of creating a more exciting and perfect life for yourself alone or with the one you love.

Your Attitude Toward Toys

The attitude toward toys is a mirror of our attitude toward our sexuality. A true connected sexuality brings the erotic home and brings the playful, sexual, sensual, fulfilling aspects of sexuality into your daily existence instead of keeping it out there at a distance.

Men may be hostile toward vibrators almost as a form of jealousy.

But I think of vibrators as helpers rather than rivals. When you add up the advantages versus the disadvantages, it is quite clear that if he or she is wise, your lover will be happy to join his partner in using a variety of toys and will become increasingly excited by them as the uninhibited results speak for themselves and are extremely gratifying when shared.

Masturbating by yourself, as opposed to with your lover, is wonderful. The better and more versatile you get by yourself, the better you get with your accepting and desirous lover. Practice makes perfect.

When you use a vibrator in the presence of your lover, you are making love and sharing your delight and joy with your beloved. You are both involved emotionally and psychologically. Your beloved is there with you because you want the experience to be a sharing of loving, and making love with each other at the same time.

Your attitude should be one of exploration and enthusiasm with your partner that allows you to develop an armamentarium of techniques and toys. Like a wardrobe of clothing, this will allow you to play different roles at different times and enjoy a variety of stimulation, giving you an enormous and immense choice of sexual activity that cannot, and should not, be ignored in any long-standing love relationship.

Everyone should have toys, just as everyone has a child inside who needs to play.

Chapter 16

How to Have
an Orgasm
If You Have
Never Had One

Most men don't have a problem having an orgasm once they have an erection, but surprising numbers of women do have trouble achieving orgasm. According to Dr. Eileen Palace of the Tulane University School of Medicine: "Orgasm disorders affect more than 23.5 million women, and desire disorders affect more than 15 million women in the United States." In desire disorders, there is an "absence or decline in interest in sexual activity with a mate or other partner, in sexual dreams and fantasies, and in reactions to people of the opposite/same sex."

Yet why should a woman go through life without experiencing the most extraordinary and exciting sensation that is possible in the human body? Why allow yourself to live a half-life, unable to know the ecstasy that so many others enjoy? Houses, boats, cars, jewels—all symbols of affluence—mean nothing since they can be sold, stolen, broken, or lost. But with health, the love of friends and family (even just one other person), and a vigorous, orgasmic sex life, you have just about everything.

If this is you, and for any one of a variety of psychological reasons you have not yet experienced orgasm, now is the time to do something about it. Give it a try and you will very likely succeed. It is nothing to be ashamed of or embarrassed about. It is something to take action on immediately.

The future is not a matter of chance. It's a matter of choice. It's not a thing to be waited for. It's a thing to be achieved.

If you can confront your sexual problems, you can confront any problems, anything.

The First Steps to Arousal

Find a quiet time in a private, secure place where you won't be interrupted by phone, fax, friends, or kids. Give yourself at least several hours and try it for several days.

1. **Examine** your body as I explain in Chapter 6. Look in the mirror without any clothes on, get comfortable, and accept your body.
2. **Look** at your genitals and say hello with your fingers coated in saliva or a lubricant.
3. **Touch** your body all over.
4. **Explore** different kinds of touch, varying the speed and pressure to see how it feels.
5. **Experiment** by stroking different parts of your body.
6. **Stroke** your underarms. Lightly brush from your armpits down the inside of your arm toward the fingertips. Then come back from your fingers and up the inside of your arm. Do this four times slowly.
7. **Do** four strokes going in the other direction from the crease of the underarm down along the side of the breast toward the abdomen.
8. **Rub** a dozen times in circles in the center of the armpit. You will find an intensely stimulating area there.

This is an extremely pleasant and relaxing way to begin to teach your mind what the first hint of arousal feels like. It is this attitude of adventure and exploration that I want you to take with you into your lovemaking as you try to have your first orgasm. Use it as a constant reminder of being connected to your mind, your body, and your spirit as you learn to understand and admire your own sexuality.

Now it is time to experiment with toys that will help you have your first orgasmic experience. (See Chapter 15 for a description of sex toys.)

Experimenting with Toys

When you have become familiar with your body and you decide to begin learning how to have an orgasm, do the following:

1. Buy a magic wand-type vibrator, a Water Dancer, or break-apart Apollo vibrator.
2. Once you have selected a few toys to try, and taken them home, it may be a few days before you unwrap and examine them. Don't force it. When you feel ready to begin your trip to having an orgasm, pick a private time when you won't be interrupted.
3. Take a bath, turn down the lights, massage yourself all over with a scented oil, sweeten the air with some essential oils.
4. Touch yourself with your vibrator. Try different spots on or around your clitoris. Be sure to lubricate your vulva with a product like Astroglide if it's dry.
5. Think exciting thoughts. Perhaps read a romance or erotic book as you use your vibrator. Maybe you would enjoy reading accounts of other women's fantasies. Nancy Friday's *Women on Top* is one example. Try anything you think might help excite you.
6. Don't tense up. Stay relaxed.

7. Place the toy over different parts of your body until you become comfortable with its sensation.
8. Then place it over the clitoral area. I recommend the electric plug-in magic wand vibrator for the beginner because this works best, is easiest to use, and is least intimidating.

Remember as you explore with your vibrator, there are very few nerve endings inside the vagina that respond to light touch or friction. Most of them respond to distension, or being stretched, and they can't be reached with a vibrator anyhow.

The first orgasm you have is almost certainly going to come from the clitoral area.

Therefore you should not use dildo-shaped vibrators or G-spot vibrators when you are beginning to explore yourself because inserting them will very unlikely be of any help for your first experience.

Also pay no attention to the claim made by some women who are experienced, that they can have an orgasm only during intercourse. I have never met a woman who is orgasmic only during intercourse and not orgasmic with manual or oral stimulation, or while playing with toys. Actually, more and more women are admitting that they cannot have an orgasm with intercourse and they need oral or manual stimulation of their clitoris. For having your first orgasm, massaging the clitoris with a toy is certainly best and will likely work.

Advice for the Male

If you are the male partner of a woman who has never had an orgasm, you should support her using a vibrator to enhance her sexual pleasure and to help her discover how to have an orgasm so she can experience this wonderful addition to life with you. Recognize how unlikely it is that she will start to have orgasms with intercourse. It is possible that she will *never* become orgasmic with intercourse. To help, you might take her vibrator and massage her genital area with it to excite her.

How to Finally Explode

Now, if you finally get aroused by yourself or with the help of your partner but you can't get over the top, what do you do?

You continue to masturbate.

Tease your clitoris with a stimulating, vibrating toy.

Then stop.

Start playing again.

Play with yourself. The vibrations of a toy will jump-start your arousal level. Take your time and relax. It's pleasure, not work. But remember some degree of muscular tension and frustration has to go along with sexual arousal.

Focus on your sensation of being aroused.

Take slow, deep breaths.

Squeeze your Love Muscles.

Relax.

Stimulate your clitoris again with a vibrator.

Spend a little time each day masturbating with your vibrators and hands, without the expectation of having an orgasm. Gradually use your Love Muscles and breathing to build yourself up. Experiment with the other toys you bought.

Remember, setting out to have your first real orgasm, it is important to be able to forget childhood restrictions and fears and to let go. Many of the women I have spoken to who have difficulty with orgasm have a problem because they are afraid of losing control. This is particularly true when they make love with a partner. Remember, as I have said, sex is not about control. It's about mutual pleasure.

So, simply let your muscles relax, think of something beautiful or some sexual fantasy that excites you, and tell yourself to unwind. Don't think about making love. Don't force anything. Just know that you are there to be happy and have fun.

Think of your arm and leg muscles as soft and flexible, like rubber bands. Slip into a semiconscious euphoria. Feel a sense of relaxed excitement, of happiness. Remember that it doesn't matter whether you have an orgasm or not, and because you are so relaxed and it feels so good, you may very well have one.

One day it will happen. A thought or movement or those rapid vibrations will suddenly shoot an orgasm your way, and you will discover one of the greatest pleasures in life—and it's free. That first orgasm will be an extraordinary shock. It is as though you are a blind person suddenly having your sight restored and seeing shapes and colors, or a deaf person suddenly hearing voices of loved ones and music.

It may be only a small sensation at first, but it will be a feeling you will never forget, and one that you will look forward to having again and again.

Water Masturbation

As you continue to learn about what brings on an orgasm, one of the most common places to experiment is in the bathroom or Jacuzzi. Many women have told me that the faucet from their tub, the jet from their bidet, the flow from a douche nozzle, a handheld showerhead, a Water Pik, or the jet from a Jacuzzi can be used to masturbate. The warmth and pressure of the water can be quite stimulating.

It's extremely important to remember some of these water jets may come out at very high velocity. A forceful stream of water inserted into the vagina may force fluid through the cervix and into the uterus and could cause pelvic infection. The result of that could be infertility and chronic pelvic pain. So, experiment with water carefully and playfully on your clitoris and labia, and you should have no trouble.

Vibrators—Addiction or Pleasure

Some people worry that they will become addicted to a vibrator and won't be able to go back to sex without it.

If you are one of those women who cannot have an orgasm with manual, oral, or vaginal stimulation, or with intercourse, and you become accustomed to a vibrator with which you have finally achieved the sublime state of orgasm, then . . . so what. You should have no fear of being dependent on this aid to orgasm. Chances are that you will continue to enjoy sex in an ever-widening variety of fashions.

A vibrator will give you the confidence and knowledge that your body is responsive and you can go on to discover new ways of playing.

I do not recommend trying to wean yourself from a vibrator. I suggest you use a vibrator as part of a natural way of loving. Do not fear it. I think it's a myth that vibrators provide sensations that are so marvelous and so sinfully gratifying that they will replace your partner or make it impossible for you to come with your partner. You may in time be able to enjoy both.

After your first orgasm, the more frequently you experience positive sexual responses, the more reliable and self-confident your sexuality will become. I urge both men and women to let go of the demands they place on themselves about having an orgasm each time they become aroused. Stop worrying about vibrator addiction and become more concerned with enjoying loving in the fullest sense of the word.

Your vibrator develops a sensory pathway from your clitoris to your consciousness. It helps you to get rid of many inhibitions that have built up that may need this more vigorous force and more significant amount of receptor nerve stimulation to break through to finally reach a level of consciousness that generates orgasm.

As long as you remember that *you* are in control of your own sexuality, that when you have an orgasm, despite the fact that your consciousness may sublimely and momentarily merge with that of the universe, you are still you.

Toys do not have minds of their own. Only you have a mind, and you are always in control.

Can a vibrator permanently numb your genitals? No.

Can they damage nerve endings? No.

They will do nothing but help you have an orgasm, and then help you and your partner to have even more heightened levels of arousal and gratification.

A good rule to keep in mind is that "if it doesn't hurt, it won't hurt you."

If it feels wonderful, it *is* wonderful.

The more aroused you get, the more arousing your actions and even bodily odors (your pheromones), are to your partner. Try letting your partner use the vibrator on you with your guidance. Remember to alternate the vibrator with your fingers, his fingers, or let him use his mouth and tongue—playful, inventive, wonderful fun.

Things that may feel uncomfortable at the beginning become more comfortable with arousal. So do not be afraid to use vibrators in places that begin to excite you but that you are not quite used to.

Men have been resistant to learning about vibrators and clitoral stimulation because they think REAL SEX for REAL MEN is a quick orgasm with the penis plunging in and out of the vagina. Therefore it is an educational process to teach your partner not only about toys but about loving and consciousness.

In my experience, about fifty percent of all women are not orgasmic with penis-vaginal intercourse alone.

So, if you have been unable to have an orgasm through vaginal-penile intercourse, don't despair.

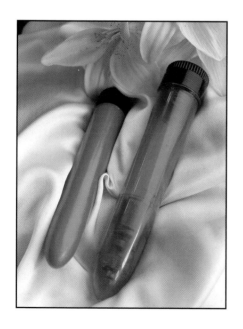

You are normal.

You are not alone.

Give yourself time, and don't be afraid.

Many of you will start having orgasms with a wand or pocket vibrator and will, after much practice, be able to *transfer* this new-found ability to have orgasms, and your new self-confidence, to having orgasmic sex with your partner. You might use your vibrator in front of him, or let him stimulate you with your special toy. First show him what you do and how to do it. Then let him help hold your vibrator. Since he can't feel how hard he is pushing on your delicate tissues, he needs your hand for guidance.

After orgasm this way is reinforced several times, try vaginal intercourse in positions that allow to use your vibrator at the same time. Whether you play with toys or body parts, if you do it together, you are having sex together.

Intercourse is a merging of hearts and minds, not just bodies.

Trying Dildos

Now, once having learned how to successfully use a magic wand vibrator for clitoral stimulation, with and without your lover's participation, and knowing that the explosive orgasm of the vibrator is basically a celebration of clitoral sexuality, you may next want to graduate to dildo-shaped vibrators for vaginal or G-spot stimulation. You must wonder about all the fuss women make about their G-spot.

Go shopping and ask for battery or plug-in vibrators with a curve to help you reach your G-spot. It is almost impossible for a woman to give herself G-spot stimulation with her fingers alone (though her partner can do it) or even with a straight vibrator. It is much easier to do this with a curved vibrator.

As you learn to experience an orgasm and then move on to bringing a vibrator or dildo into your relationship with your man, it is important to discuss it with him to get a clear understanding that he is not being replaced by an electrical or battery-powered instrument. It is simply that your love life is being enriched by a toy that brings variety and new excitement into your relationship. You may decide to tell him the truth: that you really can't have a satisfying orgasm without one.

Better yet, show him how to use the dildo and put him in charge of that one while you simultaneously use a wand on your clitoris or while you are having intercourse.

Overcoming Shyness

The use and popularity of vibrators and the ability to discuss them has increased dramatically in recent years. As more and more women learn to experience the pleasure of masturbation and nonintercourse stimulation by their partner, they are expanding their sexuality, pushing the limits beyond anything they have ever dreamed.

For the woman who has never had an orgasm, who is probably embarrassed by this fact, who feels inadequate, who may think there is something biologically wrong with her, that perhaps some vital part in her body is broken or missing, it is important for her to lose her shyness and confront the issue.

Every woman can have an orgasm.

You must open your mind and decide that you positively want this new experience. Once your mind is in the positive mode, your body will be ready to follow.

The worst that can happen is that your efforts to experiment and find the right way for you to have an orgasm won't work because you can't let go, or your fears are too deeply ingrained, or the taboo against masturbation is too strong for you to overcome alone.

In this *very rare* case, you should consult a professional for advice.

But the chances are that you will gradually find so much pleasure in the sensations you give yourself that you will wish you hadn't waited so long to try them and worried about what would happen if you did.

Now, with your newly discovered capability, you will feel at last like a whole and sexually fulfilled woman.

Anal Sex: Note

The following two chapters contain material I believe to be the last frontier of sexual exploration. They are important to a full understanding of female and male sexuality.

They discuss the option of anal sex, which some of you may have tried, others have only read or heard about, and still others are curious to be informed about.

If you do not feel ready to learn about anal sex at this time, I suggest you skip to Chapter 19. As your knowledge and experience grow, you may find that you are curious enough to explore these chapters at a later date.

Chapter 17

Anal Sex: Another Sexual Frontier

There is a very intense curiosity among men and women about anal sexuality. People are talking about it and reading about it in magazines more frequently. In my opinion, there is a tremendous hunger for accurate information in this often misunderstood area.

The Anal Taboo

The possible functions of the anus are poorly understood because most doctors and almost all women and men have difficulty accepting and getting to know more about this part of the body. It has always been shrouded in the restrictions and fears a taboo places on it.

Physicians who could and should be a valuable source of information, experience, and advice about enjoying the anus either ignore it or avoid discussion. If doctors were freed from this personal prejudice, these physicians could do a better job hearing the concerns of their patients and offering constructive suggestions as to how the anus can be experienced pleasurably with minimum risk.

For example, in proctology, the medical specialty studying the anus and rectum, there has been an almost universal reluctance to acknowledge that the anus and rectum have potential sexual or even sensual significance. In fact, I have never heard it discussed or suggested by medical specialists.

What is a taboo and why does it still affect us?

A taboo, as you probably know, is a prohibition passed down through centuries and collectively shared by a society with a force so strong that it is rarely questioned or discussed. Taboos lack all justification. They need no explanation. They are forbidden subjects no longer to be thought about. They have a quality that makes them highly resistant to logic, scientific inquiry, or even experience. A taboo just "is."

The pressures against anal enjoyment are complex, but because of them we have all suffered from a kind of psychological and social control, more influencing than even the most rigid religious control. Modern society is in the habit of believing that the scientific method has eradicated taboos and that only primitive people are still affected by such silly, restrictive fears. This is certainly not true.

We don't believe the gods are angry when a volcano erupts, but the man or woman who wishes to feel better about his or her anus, or even to derive excitement from it, will have to confront strong external and internal forces that say "Stop! Don't touch. It is smelly and dirty. It should have nothing at all to do with intimacy or sex." Yet there is evidence from repeated interviews with patients and couples over the years that suggests to me there is an increasing openness and willingness to experiment with anal sexuality among the younger and baby-boom population.

Surveys show that about twenty-five percent of people have tried anal sex in their lifetime, meaning the insertion of the penis into the anus. Considering the taboos, and lack of information, this seems like a lot. So, we find ourselves in a situation where there is no rational reason why men and women, or even scientists and doctors, when asked straightforward questions about the anus, anal pleasure, and anal sex, are unwilling or unprepared to discuss it.

Why is this so?

The Six Fears

1. **Fear of doing something "dirty."** Negative attitudes toward the anal area appear to be universally tied to concerns about cleanliness, which I discuss in more detail later. Relatively few cultures are as compulsive about cleanliness as Americans tend to be. It is commonly felt, therefore, that "cleanliness is next to godliness," and necessary for spiritual purity. The anus has become symbolic of all that is dirty and encourages feelings of disgust by focusing on its excretory functions and feces.

2. **Fear of feeling guilty.** The idea that there is a conflict between spirit and body is prevalent in some religious doctrine and serves to reinforce guilt if we become too sexually interested in our bodies.

3. **Fear of AIDS.** Anal sex has been strongly associated with the transmission of AIDS. But this should not ruin the sensual sexual enjoyment of the anus. Rather, this health crisis requires that we become even more conscious and informed about all health aspects of our sexuality. If each partner is HIV free, there is no danger whatsoever of getting AIDS.

4. **Fear of pain.**

5. **Fear that "decent" people don't do this.**

6. **Fear that enjoying anal sex-play may mean femininity, or worse, "latent homosexuality."** This idea is totally unfounded. Almost all cultures associate the idea of anal intercourse with femininity, probably because of its physiological similarity to vaginal intercourse—the insertion of the penis into a natural body cavity. With few exceptions, a man who enjoys anal

penetration may suspect himself of homosexual tendencies, since he thinks it to be the common form of sex between two men. Actually, oral sex is the far more frequent gay preference.

However, don't feel that if you enjoy oral or anal sex play, it indicates anything about your sex preference. Many of the husbands and lovers of my female patients have had some sexual experience with the anus. This does not make them homosexual or even bisexual. Understanding this, and getting a little reassurance from others, helps these straight men to enjoy their anuses and rectums without worrying that it necessarily means anything at all other than it's fun.

It seems obvious to me that the time is right to drop these fears, and to consciously discard the anal taboo for whatever reason it still lingers. There is no reason that it should exist. There is no reason to be captive to irrational destructive social control when we may choose instead positive, healing, healthy behavior.

Shedding Our Taboos

Two questions need answering.

1. **What can the role of the anal area be in healthy, self-affirming, sensual sexual activity when freed from the stranglehold of taboo?**
2. **How can people go about freeing themselves from this taboo?**

Attitudes were different when we were infants and small children. We took delight in all parts of our body. But something happened as we grew up. Parents warned us about showing too much interest in our bodies. Now we may take much less pleasure in them and some of us have become alienated from our physical selves, perhaps viewing the mind or spirit as either separate from our bodies or more important than our bodies.

For children, the discovery that the anus is considered bad or repulsive is confusing because the idea directly contradicts their pleasurable experience with bowel movements. It is thus important that women and men rediscover the anal area as a positive part of themselves, and that anal pleasure can be a positive part of life.

To overcome the taboo associated with anal sex, I suggest that you do what people have done through the ages. Be gentle, daring, and open minded. Take a chance with exploration. Primitive people, in time, learned to break certain taboos by, for example, entering the forbidden temple and finding that they were not struck dead. There was, instead, great pleasure with discovery.

As with all sex, anal sex is a private thing. Anal pleasure means different things to different people. It is usually erotic, a part of masturbating or having fun with a partner. It may be external with a finger massage, playful kissing with the lips, or teasing with the tongue. Because the lips, the tongue, and the anal opening are highly sensitive and potentially sexually excitable, it is not surprising that many people enjoy bringing the mouth and anus into intimate contact. Usually the tongue is run around the doughnutlike external anal sphincter and sometimes flicked or probed in and out before going back to the circular motion.

This is called analingus.

Or anal sex may be internal with a finger, penis, or object like a dildo inserted through the anal canal and into the rectum. And many men find it exciting to stimulate or have their partner stimulate the anal opening, lower rectum, and prostate with a vibrator.

Learning to be comfortable with your anus is like learning to be comfortable with sex in general. Anal awareness has two dimensions. First there is the individual process of self-exploration. And the second dimension involves sharing anal stimulation with a partner.

Keeping this pleasure potential in mind, you can now move on to learn more about your own body.

Anatomy of the Anus and Rectum

The anus is the external opening into the short anal canal, a tube-shaped entryway less than an inch long that leads into your rectum. The canal is sensitive in the lower two thirds to touch; however, inside the rectum it is less sensitive to touch and more to the pressure of stretching (this is why the inflatable vibrating anal butt plug is so much fun.)

Interestingly, the folds of tissue around the anal canal have a striking capacity for expansion, depending on the level of muscular tension. Many people who would like to try this form of sexual pleasure fall victim to the myth that it is impossible. They believe that anything larger than a finger, such as a penis, would simply not fit in, that pain would be inevitable and unbearable.

Just as the vagina expands to allow a baby to pass through, the anus has a similar power to stretch.

During rectal surgery under anesthesia, a person's anal muscles can be easily stretched so the surgeon's entire hand (!) can generally pass through the anal canal into the rectum.

The rectum itself is a tube-shaped structure made of loose folds of soft, smooth, mucus-producing tissue. Its length is eight or nine inches. Normally the rectum is more open and spacious than the anus. While the rectum is tubelike, it is not a straight tube, it takes two curves along its length.

Knowledge of these curves and the location of the prostate gland is essential if you are having anal intercourse or using anal toys. The lower rectum is tilted slightly toward the navel. After about three inches it curves in the opposite direction toward the backbone. A few inches later the rectum curves slightly back toward the front once again. It is the first curve and its muscular sling that can give the most trouble attempting to insert an object or penis into the rectum. (See Fig. 3 and 4.)

An object entering the rectum at an improper angle runs into the rectal wall at the first curve, causing discomfort and a natural avoidance reaction. For this reason, don't plunge straight in when you have anal intercourse. You have to gently feel your way.

Also, when an object is inserted into the rectum, pressure from insertion is perceived as an urge to go to the bathroom, which may result in the tensing of your muscles. You need to learn that this is an illusion and focus on relaxation, which is necessary to avoid discomfort and increase your pleasure.

The rectum is different sizes and shapes in different people. Therefore, inserting objects into the rectum may be easier for one person in a particular position or angle, while that same position may be difficult for another person. Anyone who states that one position or angle is best is simply giving his or her personal experience.

It is possible to have a situation where one partner is too large, or the other is too small. However, I would guess that the vast majority of situations where it is difficult to enter the anus are due to anal spasms rather than size.

Also, it is important to remember these are new sensations. If you've never tried playing with your butt, you are not accustomed to this type of feeling, so it may take some getting used to, which is normal.

Since the inside of the rectum has few nerve endings, aside from stretching sensations, the pleasure some people feel from deep anal thrusting is probably a response to total body contact and the emotional satisfaction from this level of intimacy.

Rectal stimulation with the penis is called by a variety of names. I use the term "anal intercourse" to describe the penetration through the anus into the rectum by the man's penis.

Anal pleasure, with or without anal intercourse, can be a comfortable part of the sensual and sexual experience of any man or woman who wants it, since the anus is one of the most sensitive areas of the body and has great sensual potential. Many women and men enjoy the sensation of feeling the anus contracting around an object such as a finger, vibrator, or penis. If you are playing with the anus, you must be sure to clip your fingernails very short and file them very smooth or use a flexible latex glove.

A Unique Opportunity

When a woman engages in anal sex with her male partner, this form of play allows her many options for delving inside her partner's body, which she otherwise would not be able to explore and allows him a chance to experience a series of new sensations.

Anal sex is the only way a woman can penetrate her lover so that he can know what it is like to be erotically entered. She can feel the same control, power, and thrill that he feels when his penis enters her. And he can know how she feels when he does it.

With anal sex you bring your partner inside you both spiritually and emotionally in order to share a joy that really extends beyond the individual to a higher consciousness. This concept of being inside your partner is symbolic of the loving and sharing I am emphasizing in this book.

Getting to Know the Prostate

Though rarely discussed, stimulating and massaging the prostate gland is important. You hear an awful lot about the trouble men have with their prostate gland as they age, how it enlarges and keeps them awake at night having to urinate at all hours. But you really never hear about the great pleasure to be had from this gland. The technique of **prostatic massage** is similar to rubbing your clitoris while having vaginal intercourse.

The significance of prostate massage in anal pleasure cannot be overemphasized. When the man is aroused, the blood vessels within the prostate gland become engorged, the surrounding prostate muscles tense, and participate in the general Love Muscle spasm of orgasm. As I have pointed out, this may have a role in reducing the incidence of prostate enlargement and helping to prevent prostate cancer. It increases the blood circulation, which carries away accumulated metabolic toxins and free radicals.

Usually the prostate cannot be as easily felt by the man as by his partner. It is most easily felt during arousal, when it becomes swollen with blood, expands in size, and becomes firm and round rather than soft and flat. Almost all of the fluid or semen is produced by the prostate gland and therefore ejaculation occurs when the muscles surrounding this gland undergo spasms. Prostate massage at this time can be *extremely* exciting.

There is nothing equivalent to the prostate in women.

Finding the Prostate

To find the prostate gland, the woman should insert a well-lubricated finger up into the man's rectum, which should be seen as a tunnel leading to a rich reward that will excite him erotically.

Now, with your partner on his back, turn your hand with your palm up and follow the inside of the rectum, moving your finger forward in the come-hither motion. It is the same motion he uses when he finds your G-spot.

As you do this, you should feel something like a soft, flattened walnut or slightly larger-size bump, which is the prostate gland. Soft at first, it is exquisitely sensitive and, with stimulation, when his excitement builds, it becomes progressively more firm.

Arousing the Prostate

A gentle circular motion around this gland and tapping your finger against it is extremely arousing and results in a unique combination of sensations. Take care to progress slowly and with a good deal of feedback from your partner. By visual and verbal communication, he should let you know what feels good and when to stop. The in-and-out insertion of a dildo feels good to a man due to the stretching/contracting of the highly innervated anal opening as well as the massaging, rubbing, and vibrating stimulation of the prostate gland.

Anal Spasms

Sexual pleasure, when fulfilled, is seen as having the potential to enhance a person's self-esteem as well as his or her relationship with others. This is impossible in a situation of fear. Thus, once you decide to accept your anus as a sexual organ, you must move carefully, gently, and slowly, so as not to cause yourself or your partner any pain. When anal pleasure is prevented by aggressive probing and forced penetration, the anal muscles go into spasms, which can make it impossible for the muscles to relax.

An **anal spasm** is an involuntary contraction of the anal sphincter muscles and is the main reason people beginning to experiment with this form of sex may have problems. Spasms not only prevent comfortable insertion but in time tend to reduce all pleasurable sensations and the ability to enjoy them.

Anal spasms can be eliminated and the capacity to enjoy anal stimulation learned even by those with a long history of difficulty enjoying sex in this area.

The most important factor in the successful management of anal spasm is the willingness to devote regular attention to anal exploration, to allowing your anal sphincter, which is under your voluntary control, to become used to being lovingly touched and then *gently* penetrated. To start, remember to *press* gently with the fleshy part of your lubricated index finger. Wait patiently until you feel the sphincter relax and open. Then slowly insert your finger. If you carry this out with calm persistence, you will succeed. If you practice, you don't have to hurt.

The Importance of Exercises

Now, to learn about your anal and pelvic muscles, you will want to locate the important ones and start a program of exercise to enhance their tone, elasticity, and sensitivity.

There are ringlike muscles that surround the anal opening. These are the anal sphincters. These muscles are capable of functioning under voluntary control. The anal sphincter muscles are part of the Love Muscles that I have described in Chapter 14. How to exercise them is also explained there.

The more intense and frequent are your anal Love Muscle contractions, the stronger your orgasms will be and the more pleasurable. It may make the difference between an earthbound orgasm and an intergalactic trip.

The anal alternative can be medically safe, intellectually stimulating, experientally new, and full of discovery and pleasure. It can be a stepping-stone to a higher level of intimate communication between loving partners and can offer a much more varied, enriched menu of delightful sexual options.

Chapter 18

Delving Further
into Anal Sex

Even if you have been fortunate enough to escape childhood warnings, most people from time to time find themselves teetering on the edge of indecision in a war between their sense of prudishness or a wish to behave properly, and the intellectual desire to be sexually liberated. The woman wants to be pure, sweet, innocent, and loving, yet at the same time she, as well as her partner, wants her to be wild, spontaneous, and exuberant in her sexuality.

Many people who would like to try something new are too embarrassed to bring it up. However, it is all right to discuss these subjects with your partner. As a matter of fact, talking about it is the only way to deal with such opposing emotional conflicts in this silent inner battle. **This communication is particularly important, since one's partner may be caught in the same set of conflicting desires.**

Anal Tension

There is little likelihood that anal intercourse will become pleasurable unless the partners have become comfortable with the idea of anal sex and have tried it by themselves.

Intimacy of body cannot come before intimacy of mind and heart if you are to reach the heights of eroticism I am suggesting. This world of erotic loving is a world of the highest and most refined artistic sensitivity and beauty.

Since your body and mind are in a constant state of interrelationship in any situation of stress, for example, the natural tendency of your body is to defecate, getting rid of all excess weight. Animals and human infants exhibit this spontaneous defecation reaction in response to fear.

However, as a result of toilet training, we learn that this response is inappropriate. Therefore, when adults are under stress, their natural response is to tighten their anuses in an effort to counteract the urge to defecate. That is why most adults learn to associate a tense anus with fear (this is called tenesmus).

The anal response to fear is instinctive. But you learned from society how to control your response. Because you have learned it, you are not stuck with it for life. You can simply unlearn it. You just have to want to.

The key to dealing with anal tension is to understand the reasons behind it.

You can't force your anus to relax, but as you give it more attention, it will gradually relearn to be more and more at ease, more accustomed to pleasurable activity, and less and less surprised by the positive responses it is getting from your brain. The following exercise will assist you in this.

Techniques for Exploration

1. Take a leisurely bath or shower. Feel the warm water against your skin.
2. As you wash, make each stroke slow and sensuous.
3. Gently and thoroughly wash your anus.
4. After bathing, squat over a lighted makeup mirror to see your anus.
5. Now touch and stroke the outside of the anus in a circular fashion, allowing the doughnut-shape anal sphincter muscle to relax.
6. If it tenses up, place your finger with gentle, steady pressure on the sphincter muscle. It will become used to being touched and will eventually relax.
7. Close your eyes and breathe deeply and slowly as you become conscious of your anus.

Anal masturbation is one of the best ways to learn more about your body and expand your capacity for erotic pleasure. It can be enjoyed with simultaneous clitoral, vaginal, or penile stimulation. Once you are able to please yourself, you can show your partner how to please you. If you do it in front of your partner, you may involve him or her by having them put their hand on your thigh or tummy.

Undistracted by others, you can concentrate completely on what gives you pleasure. Some people get so focused on coming that they fail to enjoy the process of getting there. Masturbation is fun and it doesn't have to lead anywhere. Fantasy is fun, too, and bears no relation to things people would actually do. So you can fantasize with your anus as well as your clitoris, or your penis, or any other part, whatever pleases your heart and head.

Let your mind wander, thinking over recent sexual experiences.

Let your mind focus on one sexual experience where your partner wanted to put a finger on or inside your anus, if that has happened.

Now remember a time when a partner wanted to have or actually had anal intercourse with you or inserted a sex toy into your anus, if you had such an experience and it was a positive one.

As you consider and remember these things, you will realize that during every experience that was positive, you were accepting your body and your anus. During every experience that was negative, you were essentially rejecting your body and your anus or rejecting the pain associated with an overeager, overaggressive, or anally inexperienced lover. You will find that your body remembers. If you allow anal sex that is repeatedly painful, it will cause an increase in tension that will be progressively more difficult to deal with.

When you approach anal sex with the lingering memory of pain, your anus becomes tight because you are naturally apprehensive, but you may decide to go ahead anyhow. Your anal muscles tense to repel the uncomfortable invasion. However, with continued force, the muscles give up. They can resist no longer. And if no physical damage is done by this forcible entry, such as a tear, after a while the pain does go away, but the memory of pain is reinforced.

In this drama, your anus never really feels comfortable, and at best it is in a state of neutral toleration. Real pleasure occurs once you give up the idea of force.

You must never deliberately submit your anus, penis, clitoris, or vagina to any pain. This rule is the foundation of sexual pleasure.

Never see your anus as a passive receiver of sex but, rather, as an active player in a mental and emotional adventure.

You must learn how to enhance pleasurable experiences and avoid ever having unpleasant ones.

It is impossible for a person to be anally active unless he or she feels a real sense of safety. Know that your partner won't hurt you, that he or she will stop when asked, that you feel comfortable with his or her judgment, patience, and cleanliness. That they won't discuss your private sex life with others. This will help give you confidence to relax.

It is impossible to abandon oneself to play without this sense of safety. When we feel comfortable, we can let down our protective barriers. You can give up control even though you are not sure what is going to happen. This can be done only in a very trusting relationship, which is earned, not forced.

As you begin to explore your anus, you should remember that your anal canal and rectum do not ordinarily store any solid masses of fecal material. The rectum and anal canal are passageways.

I think the intense feeling of revulsion that is commonly associated with feces goes far beyond a concern for hygiene. It reflects a fundamental ambivalence toward the body's natural functions. One way in which our culture expresses its traditional mistrust of the body is through its relentless efforts to cover up or eliminate all natural odors and secretions.

Once you give up the fear of discovering feces in your rectum, which should not be there, you can discard the idea that your anus was made only for poop and start welcoming this part of you for pleasure. There is nothing inherently dirty about the anal opening.

Bathing is usually adequate for cleaning this area, especially when you learn to feel comfortable putting your finger in your anus as part of taking a shower. Bathing together and washing each other's genital and anal areas can be a bonding, intimate, as well as loving exchange. Germs such as E. coli and other sorts of natural anal bacteria can cause problems. If you just exercise regular common-sense cleanliness you can prevent the unintentional transportation of these organisms on your fingers, a toy, or your penis.

Try keeping a candle, a bowl of warm, soapy water, and a dry hand towel next to your bed. It's a romantic reminder that cleanliness and loving work together.

Peter's Problem

Regular and careful washing can leave your anal area fresh and clean. However, people may not be aware that their anal area is not perhaps as clean as it should be, or that there is stool present in the lower rectum, which should be evacuated.

I recall the case of Jenny, who complained about her husband, Peter's total insensitivity and carelessness with regard to anal hygiene. Jenny enjoyed all forms of sexual behavior, including anal sex play. But she was turned off by Peter's inadequate cleansing of this area. His morning showers were rushed, he often went to the bathroom during the day and never showered before bed at night.

Rather than give up sex with a part of him she loved as well as she loved him, she took matters into her own hands and regularly used soap, water, and a washcloth to wash his butt like a baby's behind before playing with it. Despite open communication, she could never get the point through to him that she would prefer he take care of this himself. Perhaps he liked the feeling of having her do it. Since she didn't mind, it didn't matter.

Remember, partners should never insert a finger, penis, or anything else in the vagina after direct contact with the anus because the vagina can easily catch a variety of infections from the germs in and around the anus. This is by no means inevitable, however it is possible and one should always be careful.

Continuing to Explore

1. Now that you have examined your anus in a lighted mirror, try inserting your lubricated finger or dildo into the anal canal and rectum. You will feel like you have to go to the bathroom. If this happens, reassure yourself and say, "No, there's nothing there," and just relax.
2. Move your finger in and out slowly until you are comfortable and familiar with the sensation. Be sure it is well lubricated with Vaseline.

    Remember that unlike the erection of the penis,

which happens automatically when aroused, the ability to relax the anus is something that must be practiced and learned.

3. **When your finger is in your anus as far as you want it to go, stop there and let your anal muscles get used to the presence of your finger. Your anus will begin to relax when it discovers this is not an invasion but a friendly expedition.**

4. **Breathe slowly and deeply. Each time you repeat this exercise, you will find that your finger will comfortably go in a little more.**

5. **Move your finger slowly in a circular motion.**

6. **Stop before you feel uncomfortable.**

    Soon you will be able to put your finger all the way inside your anal canal. You will be entering the lower rectum, which will feel soft and open.

7. **Experiment with moving your finger in and out, back and forth, and around in a circle.**

This exploration inside your anus can be a turning point in your desire for anal pleasure.

Now you are ready to experiment with your partner. If you are anxious during mutual exploration of the anus, tell your partner how you feel. You can try alternating. First you try it. Then he tries it.

If you are uncomfortable, stop what you are doing. *Wash your hands and fingers carefully.* Do something new. Remember you can always come back to something you stopped when you are ready.

Express your feelings while you are having them.

Plan for extensive foreplay around the anal sphincter during which you ask your partner not to attempt to insert his penis. For the moment you are just experimenting with anal pleasure.

Your partner may lose his erection, but that's okay, he'll gain it back soon enough with reassurance. He or she may also expel some gas at inopportune moments. Whether fart or vart, such unavoidable natural occurrences are best accepted with a laugh and a shrug.

Health Considerations

When he does have an erection, and you feel comfortable having anal intercourse, he should put on a condom unless you are in a monogamous, committed relationship and you are sure he is disease free. How can you be certain?

If you are starting a new relationship and you both are not going to have any other sexual partners but you have had them in the past, then you should both have a blood test that includes syphilis, gonorrhea, HIV, chlamydial cultures, and a medical examination to detect venereal warts and other genital problems.

Ideally, you should use condoms for six months, then repeat the tests. If they are again negative, you can eliminate the use of condoms for the duration of your relationship, as long as both partners remain monogamous. I suggest condoms for six months because the tests may take six months to become positive, so that if your girlfriend or boyfriend made love yesterday to someone with HIV the test tomorrow would be negative.

Even in monogamous relationships the male must urinate (to flush the urethra) and wash his penis thoroughly after anal intercourse to minimize the risk of E. coli or other natural rectal organisms causing a bladder or prostate infection. This careful penile washing also protects his lover from vaginal infections with the same rectal organisms. Use of condoms for anal intercourse is always safest. Analingus may transmit GI parasites and other oral fecal-transmitted germs. Knowing your partners activities and having meticulous anal hygiene must be regularly practiced precautions.

Anal Intercourse

To begin:

1. Apply Vaseline to his penis as well as around and in your anal opening.
2. Select the most comfortable position for both of you.
3. Put his penis head gently against your anus while you breathe deeply.
4. Stay in this position while you relax.
5. Then gently bear down with your anal muscles, pushing as though you were about to have a bowel movement.
6. Ask him to move the head of his penis gently into your anus as you allow your anal and rectal Love Muscles to let go and relax.
7. Once his penis is inside, ask him to be completely still until you become accustomed to the sensation.
8. Then tell him which movement you find most pleasurable.
9. Start with slow movements. Do not try vigorous motion.

Once in your anus, his erection may again come and go somewhat. This is natural, because even though the anal sphincter may seem relaxed, it still can be quite tense and reduce or strangle the blood flow to the penis. But as you become comfortable that what you are doing is not painful, the muscles will relax, you can begin slow in-and-out movement, the blood flow to your lover's penis will increase, and his penis will once again become hard.

During this first experience be sure to be direct, stating what you want clearly. Don't be shy or vague or use double meanings.

Some people say their partners automatically start thrusting deeply as soon as they insert themselves. They soon learn that neither of them derives any pleasure from such vigorous motion. Gentle motion is exciting, and you can create very intense and loving sexual sensations, as I have described earlier, by contracting and relaxing your Love Muscles with hardly any movement of your pelvis at all. Once the penis is in your anus, just contract and relax. Relax with insertion. Contract with withdrawal. Increase your rhythmic pace as arousal and comfort progress.

Some partners will enjoy receiving intercourse for a few minutes, others for longer. There is no such thing as "should" during loving. Whatever feels good and most pleasurable must be communicated to your partner, and neither one should feel compelled to do anything he or she does not want to do.

Stimulus Sharing

In advising people about anal intercourse, I frequently recommend a technique called Stimulus Sharing.

When two stimuli—for example, anal and clitoral massage—are associated because they are done together repeatedly, they become linked. Thus, by using a fantasy about your clitoris that is really exciting with stimulation of the anus, which did not excite you before, the two become locked in your mind.

You can arouse yourself with an already proven method of clitoral stimulation using a toy or your hand, whichever really excites you, and once aroused, you can gradually introduce anal play. This will associate clitoral excitement with anal touching, and then anal touching alone with sexual pleasure. In time you can condition yourself to respond erotically to stimulation of your anus alone.

Men can do the same thing by stimulating or masturbating their erect penis at the same time as they explore their anus.

By the way, women can also use this conditioning technique by exciting the clitoris and touching their nipples at the same time.

Some can do this until they reach the point where nipple stimulation alone can give them an orgasm.

You may now be ready to try toys designed especially for anal-rectal stimulation.

Butt Plugs

One example of such a toy is called a Butt Plug. (See Chapter 15 for photographs.) Once inserted in the anus, a butt plug is designed to stay in place even while you engage in other sexual activities. Butt plugs, as all toys, are available in different shapes and sizes and can be used by men or women. As you use this toy on yourself, before you have your partner use it on you, ask yourself as you have done before, "Are the sensations I am experiencing uncomfortable or just different?" If uncomfortable, then back off. Usually the sensations are just different and you need to think of fantasies that relax you and allow you to continue your anal explorations up to, during, and after orgasm.

There are many other types of butt plugs such as an electric vibrating butt plug, a battery-operated vibrating butt plug, and a vibrating butt plug that is surrounded by a balloon-type mechanism with a bulb that blows up like a blood pressure cuff. You insert the well-lubricated plug into your anus, then squeeze the bulb as though you were taking your blood pressure, and the part in the rectum blows up like a small balloon.

This is intensely stimulating since the rectum and prostate respond to pressure and stretching more than they do to direct touching. This toy is a little hard to find but is available.

Anal Beads

There are beads, usually a string of four to six in various sizes, that can be inserted into the anus of a man or woman. They are attached to a loop on the end, held outside.

The idea here is that when you are just about to have your orgasm, or during the orgasm, your partner pulls the beads out quickly, which results in intense stimulation and a soaring arousal to the orgasm in progress. Beads connected by cotton string are impossible to properly clean. Obtain ones that are completely plastic and washable.

Men and Vibrators

Powerful sensations from anal use of dildos, plugs, and vibrators have been reported to be very effective in male sexual stimulation. However, few can say they are able to climax with a vibrator applied to the penis alone. In fact, most men would rather play with a "soft-on" than try to put a vibrator on their limp penis. The common reaction from men is "It was too fast," "It just didn't feel good," "I couldn't get hard," "I couldn't come," "I actually got numb." This is not the case, however, when using anal stimulation.

Most men would enjoy prostate massage during sex play and orgasm. With your finger you can feel the muscles surrounding the prostate throb and pulsate with ecstatic spasms as the fluid of ejaculation surges out of the penis. Stimulation of the anal sphincter, stimulating the sensitive nerves surrounding the prostate gland, and distending the rectum with a finger or dildo, can give extraordinary pleasure to your male partner.

The Freedom to Talk

A recent article in *Playboy* said that "anal sex is the greatest thing going," and many would agree. With the right preparation and care, anal sex can provide immense pleasure for a couple and also build intimacy. Those who have never before included their anuses in erotic play are usually able to do so comfortably once they exchange direct permission from their partners.

Quite clearly we have liberalized our attitude toward anal sexual activity at least to the point where we can bring it up among more and more people, though not everyone, as a subject for objective discussion. Some still think "nice" people don't discuss such subjects. I disagree.

Nice people are open-minded and willing to share all natural body parts, positions, and places with their lovers.

Nice people talk to each other.

Nice people do not have trouble making explicit requests, saying what they like and what they don't like, what they like better and what they like less.

Nice people do not have partners who are victims, but partners who are truly partners.

Nice people let themselves say no. They learn to divert behavior that feels like it should be a no until a later point when it feels like it should be a yes.

In sex, as with everything, it's impossible for a person to say yes to anything unless he or she feels the complete freedom to say no.

All of the suggestions here can help you to become more creative. To get the most out of these possibilities, you and your partner must agree to talk and share responsibility for your pleasure instead of trying to read each other's minds. To do this, you must develop trust in your partner's capacity to take care of him or herself and to accept you as you are. You also need to develop great ease in accepting differences in personal preferences, and being totally non-manipulative in your communication.

In contrast, if you and your partner abandon contact with your minds and spirits, then touching can become alienating. And the more intimate the touching is, the more alienating and fear-producing it will be.

This is because anal stimulation is probably the most emotion-laden aspect of sexuality.

If you are seen as manipulative by your partner, in other words, you are trying this not because you both agree but because he or she is insisting, you are very likely not going to be able to share this very delightful part of human sexuality with abandon and freedom.

Thus it is important that you be in full contact with yourself, heart, mind, body, and spirit, in order for you to be in full contact with your partner's heart, mind, body, and spirit. You must feel secure in all respects so you can be erotic, sensual, and exploratory. Then what happened to Allison when she licked chocolate from her husband's anus in Chapter 13 might happen to you. There was an explosion of unexpected pleasure rather than uncertainty about what she was doing.

Drugs and Anal Eroticism

People have always looked for substances that can alter their sexual experiences in some desired way. I'm sure that at some point you have heard claims that anal relaxation or erotic highs can be obtained from using any of five types of drugs: alcohol, marijuana, cocaine, volatile nitrates such as "poppers," and the street drug called Ecstacy.

I will limit my comments only to say that if a glass of wine will help you relax and focus on pleasurable sensations from your body or your anus, I can think of no reason for not having one. On the other hand, the regular *necessity* to use more than one glass of wine to enjoy yourself sexually, or to use drugs that are habit-forming, addicting, or life-threatening, is simply ridiculous.

The use of lubricants containing topical anesthetic ointments like zylocaine is primarily motivated by the desire to reduce anal pain. Anal pain that persistently accompanies the insertion of a finger, penis, or toy signals the need for patience and relaxation, practice, or indicates a medical problem.

The mind is your best ally. If, for example, *after* penile insertion occurs, the anal muscles spasm, withdraw and try a second time when your partner indicates she or he is relaxed and ready. You will be amazed what results accrue from such thoughtful consideration. If two tries fail, try again another day.

A Double Purpose

Look, then, upon your anus as a part of your body that has a double purpose, just as the vagina and penis have. They are passages through which you evacuate waste. And they are passages through which you receive intense excitement.

Other parts of the body have several uses also. For example, just as your tongue helps in eating, it is also essential for speech.

We are not simply child-making vehicles. We are constructed to receive an enormous amount of pleasure with kissing, licking, massaging, and sexual playing of all types. If these sensitive nerves are there, they should certainly be used to make life more enjoyable and positive. Otherwise the body would be like a piano with a whole section of keys missing. How sad that would be for the lover of music. How sad it would be for loving couples if parts of our bodies were rejected out of fear or ignorance.

The miracle of our bodies is that so many nerves in so many places are open to erotic stimulation. Sexual partners can learn a great deal about themselves and each other if they are willing to take the risks of self-exploration and share themselves with delight and confidence as well as accept their lover with an open heart.

The idea of getting permission from your partner is very important. Sex is not a battlefield for determination of control issues. It's not a control drama. It's not about power or who is the dominant force in a relationship.

Sex is not the stage on which gender power games should be played. Loving is a pleasure-oriented encounter. It is not performance oriented.

Loving should not be hard work. It should be fun.

Loving should be an opportunity to explore ever new horizons in a world that is limited only by your imagination.

It is important, then, to see your anus as an active participant in the psychological/spiritual/emotional event of loving rather than as a passive receptacle for the toleration of sexual activities that are gratifying only to your partner.

So enjoy yourself. All of yourself.

To love well is to live well.

Part Four

A New Beginning
for the
Third Millennium

Chapter 19

The Value of Change

When high-performance athletes play a sport, they are psycho-physically so integrated that they are no longer aware of the voluntary directions they give to their muscles. They are no longer conscious of technique. They don't have to think in order to act in an optimum way.

Going with the Flow

There is an integrated natural flow. It happens, for example, in swimming when you put one hand over the other, kick your feet, and you have a goal that you are working toward. You're trying to get to the end of the pool. You're fulfilling your goal as you go. Spontaneously and without thought you move your hands and feet through the water because it really has become second nature.

You are going with the flow.

Or it is like playing a tennis match. Once you know how to hit a good backhand and forehand, you can play the game for fun. If you don't know how, the activity is continually draining your energy because you must constantly think, "How do I hit this forehand?" Or, "Where should I go to hit the ball?" But once learned, the game becomes automatic. You are there where the ball is at the right moment.

This is the concept of spontaneous right action.

That is, action that occurs as if it were previously scripted. It's spontaneous only after years have been devoted to mastering technique. Thus it is really spontaneous only after you are already wonderful at it. It is right because you have thought about it over and over, and with mastery you become progressively less dependent on thinking.

Because some people have trouble with sex all the time, and most people have problems with sex some of the time, it is clear that sexual complexities are almost universally present in our society. There is the need to master enough technique and openness of attitude so that right sexual actions become second nature. You are no longer thinking about each step. You are participating as a whole being. When your lovemaking proceeds with flow, you've reached the point when you know you can make your whole life and your relationship healthier, more joyous, and long-lasting.

You naturally plan for sexual evenings full of love and desire. You do things that are affectionate and loving and completely spontaneous, without premeditation. You may find it exhilarating to make love in unusual places. Bring a spirit of adventure. **Create memories of love that last for years to come.**

Your values and spirit guide you infallibly to spontaneous right actions. You've overcome many problems in your sexuality and the limitations in your consciousness. You've practiced and become skilled. And with that skill you've become the equivalent of a high-performance athlete. Your hands slice the water effortlessly. You hit the right stroke. It's the right place.

Sexuality may be the most sensitive, difficult area you have ever tackled, but it is also easiest in the sense that it is common to all human beings, and one area where we all have the potential to learn.

We cannot all be proficient in golf or playing the stock market, but everybody can become skilled in knowing themselves and their own sexuality.

You have the opportunity, regardless of who you are, where you are in life, or what your economic status is, to become expert in your sex life.

Finding New Energy—Moving Up the Staircase

This guide has supplied more than answers. It has taught you how to think imaginatively. It has given you a myriad of suggestions about how you can be creative in your sexuality, new ideas that put you on a path toward being your best. But once you are on that path, it's just a matter of using your newfound skills to continue to make your relationship fulfilling, your love life full of happiness, reward, and gratification, enveloping you in overflowing loving abundance, an abundance that manifests itself in taking you step by step up the energy staircase.

In your daily life, you are either gaining energy by climbing up the energy staircase, or losing energy by slipping downward. You cannot stay still. Staying still loses energy. As all your relationships flourish with the energy you have gained from your improved loving sexuality, and you successfully apply the techniques you have learned in this arena to other parts of your life, each time you are successful, it will give you even more energy. . . .

I envision moving up the staircase to mean the life energy you gain by ascending to ever higher levels of mental and spiritual evolution. As you move higher, your energy increases, the energy necessary to focus, produce change, and accomplish things.

As you progress up the staircase:

1. You gain the energy that was used to maintain (and no longer is necessary) repression, suppression, denial, guilt, resentment, and anger.

2. You gain the energy that was spent on stress you no longer have.

3. You gain energy experiencing joy and pleasure in life.

4. You gain energy from doing it right, which makes you feel better about yourself.

5. You gain energy from your lover because your improvement in sex, communication, and intimacy comes back to you in the form of enhanced love, support, encouragement, and commitment.

Thus your consciousness level and your spiritual level keep going up while your body gets healthier and more resistant to illness. The more you succeed, the more you will succeed. The more positive things you bring into life, the more positive things are attracted to you. Each time you make good things happen and recognize that you can do things, you gain psychic and spiritual energy and physical health.

By the time you have finished this book, the total enjoyment of existence will be within your reach. You have learned by doing and trying. Your success makes you more adventurous. As you gain a sense of value and respect for yourself, you enhance your valuing and respect for those around you.

Your life is full of achievement because you have confidence.

Your success in expanding the boundaries of your loving sexuality has taught you that not only can you be healthier and happier, you are able to take charge of yourself and you will find that you begin to reevaluate the events, circumstances, and activities in your life. When you have this self-possession, a number of things happen:

1. You become fully aware because you have learned respect for your mind and reverence for your body and the extraordinary powers of which you are capable.

2. You gain the ability to improve not only your loving sexuality but everything you do.

3. People see you as upbeat and happy. They notice you. Your brightness, your attractiveness, draws others who are also bright and attractive. Any depression you may have felt is a thing of the past because you relate to the positive aspects of your whole being.

4. You have found a better love life for yourself and you are aware there is an even more rewarding life just around the corner.

5. You have direction.

6. You have learned how to learn. How to visualize, focus, and create.

7. You will be able to continue on a path that makes your life richer and more fun.

Staying Younger

So, as you get older, you get better, and as you get better, you rejuvenate. You feel younger and maintain a young frame of mind. You are not set in concrete, fixed in your ideas.

You are growing and changing, and you therefore taste the excitement of a life that is vibrant and electric instead of sitting back and waiting for illness and, ultimately, death.

Don't let getting older in years affect you. You can stay forever healthier and younger in spirit if you continue to have exciting love and sex.

With your new self-awareness and self-respect from living what you have learned, you are totally in tune to those true values that lead you to the heart of life, to spiritual existence.

Now you live in the moment.

When I say you live in the moment, I mean you are mentally alive here and now, every moment you are awake and conscious. You think logically because you are better organized. You are better organized because you have learned to use the energy excess you have created to focus.

Now you focus on what you are doing. When you are at work, you are thinking about work. When you are at lunch, you are thinking about the taste of your food. You have learned to zero in on the here and now of life.

Work

You enjoy your job by valuing your work. Place a value on your time and effort. Value it because you are there in every way and it feels good to live what you believe and to believe that the work you do is worthwhile. You find renewed commitment to do your job well, to accomplish new projects and new goals by visualizing what it is you want and bringing newfound energy and focus to accomplish your goals.

Your sexual satisfaction spills over to your work life even when you have a job that does not provide you with as much gratification as you would like. Every success you have reinforces self-esteem and takes you one more step up the ladder of health, happiness, and longevity.

Children

You find closeness with your children by treating them with respect and valuing them as individuals. You praise their talents, support their natural skills, and encourage them to become the best they can be at whatever it is they decide to make of themselves. You find it easier to overlook the trivial and focus on a healthy relationship. And you find that because you are totally there when you are with your children, their demands diminish. Quality time removes the necessity of giving them burdensome quantities of time. Lessons from the kibbutz in Israel taught us long ago that one hour of directed, focused attention with your child is healthier than a whole day of their just being tolerated.

Friends

You form strong friendships with people who are happy to be with you because your aura gives them optimism and energy. They sense a profound change in you, in the shine of eyes that see dewdrops on a blade of grass, and vision that sees profound truths. You glow with happiness in yourself, in your life, in your activities. People want to be around you because your knowledge draws them to you like a magnet. Your life vitality attracts new friends who share a desire to make a difference. You encourage and nourish intimacy with friends just as you did with your lover.

Parents

You enjoy your parents, who have known you longer than anyone. You are self-confident and therefore able to admit both the good and bad in yourself as well as others without being threatened or diminished. You accept responsibility for your own life and appreciate your parents' life.

In asserting yourself you may threaten the position or role of your parents, who may be accustomed to influencing you. That's OK. It is to the spiritual/mental/physical reality of your own self that you must be true. Hopefully, your parents will be inspired by your freedom from stress and success in life to themselves take a step toward rediscovering their own vital sexuality, which exists at every age.

One is never too old for sexual pleasure and joy in life.

Community

You are admired in your community because you are becoming more involved. You have learned not only to participate and take responsibility for your sex, but also for your life. You have decided not to turn your responsibilities over to others.

People who connect to all of the above—work, children, friends, parents, and community—are close to the heart of life. These are people who will find deep, true, and lasting health, happiness, and love.

What I have done is to help you take your own sexuality as it relates to the most encompassing perceptions of life and love and by providing techniques beyond just giving you the skills to enjoy your life and relate to those around you. I have made you so aware of yourself that you are able to learn and change. Skills alone don't do it. A *skilled* disconnected person can be just as miserable as an *unskilled* disconnected person. Both are cut off from themselves.

The point you must take away with you is that the concepts you have been given are not just about how to have better sex but how to be happier, healthier, and live together longer *because* you are having better sex.

You have learned how to create an environment that is conducive to personal growth, how to make the choices that reflect your values and are consistent with who and what you are. Sexuality in this sense elevates you spiritually in every part of your life. If you learn to use this fundamental, primary energy, you are capturing an inestimable source of power to take you to ever higher and higher levels of health and joy.

By allowing yourself to discover and enjoy new things in your sex life, you become receptive to all sorts of enriching ideas and activities. By living your values and striving to do your best, you are the inspiration for your wife when she feels down, or your husband when he's disenchanted, or your children, who need someone to look up to.

You become inspiriting to others.

How you change depends on where you are coming from. Some people may not have a significant other in their lives at the moment, and they still will be changed. They too will learn how the single greatest contribution you can make to your own existence is to get your mind/spirit linked to your actions.

If you get tuned in to your loving, you really are getting tuned in to your living.

You cannot be sexually connected unless you are in touch with your own existence as a human being. We are not pure spiritual entities. We're not pure physical entities. And we're not pure mental entities, consciousness floating out there without form or substance. We are in fact physical bodies with a conscious self-awareness of our existence, with a mind that perceives and processes, and with a spirit that connects us to God and the Universe . . .

Chapter 20

Loving for the
New Millennium

I am proposing a new sexual Naissance, a new kind of consciousness. These chapters have demonstrated the tools and techniques to
help you integrate your loving sexuality to yourself and to all other
areas of life. Sexual connecting is the model and the catalyst to
speed you on.

As you've read, you have gone through the nuts and bolts of how
you can expand your sexuality. The experience you had living
through the process of visualization, taking charge of yourself, and
the changes and maturing that occurred should have resulted in a
lot of positive feedback. You should notice that it is now easier to
see the truth in yourself, the truth that comes from being able to
accept and recognize the values you cherish.

You have more energy to give to other relationships because your
personal life is more settled and stable. Your sex life has become an
expression of your exquisite, unique, and highly developed loving
sexuality. Basically something profound happened that has had a
positive impact on you.

1. You learned techniques in dealing with sexual issues
   that are usable elsewhere. You are more adventure-
   some, less fearful, more independent. You try new,

self-improving things and accomplish much by focusing your desires into intentions and your intentions into outcomes.

2. You have been successful in communing with your
   sexuality, and each new success in other areas also
   raises your energy level. Your aura expands and
   grows. Each time you deal positively with the world
   and make things happen, you reinforce your realiza-
   tion that as a result of your energy and focus, there
   are no limits to what you can accomplish.

The cost of not being involved in your sexuality is the same as the
cost of not being involved in your life. The self-confidence that
comes from truly knowing yourself sexually lets you take arms
against any type of outrageous fortune.

It is no longer "they're running the show." Now it is "my life, it's
about me, my health and happiness—what happens every day is my
responsibility."

In short, you are more in love with yourself, you respect yourself
more, and you have more confidence to fulfill your life objectives
because you have succeeded in establishing the most vital connection of all, the connection of your mind and soul to your sexuality.

Moving Upward

You are moving up the energy staircase.

1. You make time for loving. You are not speeding
   blindly in a pointless race to acquire money, fame, or
   power. You give love and are enriched by receiving
   love.
2. You take better care of your body, which you now
   cherish and know so much more intimately. It is no
   longer such a struggle to diet and exercise. You cast

away over-the-counter medications and get doctor approval to give up prescription drugs you may have been taking because you are no longer under the pressures that require them. Because you have more pleasure and less stress, your body is being exposed to less of the toxins that cause illness.

3. You begin to act on those values you never had the time for before. You are not wasting your energy dissipating it on alcohol, drugs, or pointless activity.

4. You are able to make everyone and everything around you feel better. Even your dog is happier. Children and animals no longer irritate you as much, and are drawn to you.

5. You become a more caring and giving person because in caring and giving, your life is enhanced.

6. You now take the time to notice the change of seasons, or to smell a flower, or stare endlessly at the beauty of the sky.

7. You are going to be happier as you get older and climb your staircase ever higher as you use your mind and spirit to improve your health and longevity.

We live at a time when there are few heroes to look up to anymore. Our children have lost the vision of an ideal of excellence in men and women. And so we see disintegration of the very values that form the framework upon which human spiritual evolution depends. But if you have taken the morals of this book into your consciousness and into the very fiber of your being, you will find that what you do really *does* matter.

You Are Not Limited by Anything but Your Own Mind

- You automatically become life-affirming in all of your actions.

- You elevate yourself with self-fullfillment.
- You have become resilient and strong.
- You have found sweetness in the air you breathe.

It may be that you have had to change your partner, your job, or even where you live. But the important thing is not the PLACE where you are, but the POINT where you are in your own evolution as a human being.

By being in touch with your sexuality and loving, you have learned how to live. You know all the moves, and it becomes second nature for you to choose events, circumstances, people, places, things, and activities that are healthy and healing.

- You don't have to think about how to relate. You will feel it when you are supposed to.
- You choose right living, right action, right thinking, right spirituality, right loving. It is instantaneous and intuitive.

It simply flows.

- Through your mind, you rule your body. You choose your own destiny of health, happiness, and longevity.
- You are in control of yourself.

And the life you choose today is the history you create for the future.

Take a step up the staircase, and then another, and another, and another. . . . Your energy gets higher and your health gets better as you progressively embrace your own Vital Connection between mind, spirit, and sexuality.

Index